INFORMATION MANAGEMENT

ANTECEDENTS AND CONSEQUENCES

MR AHMED RIAHI-BELKAOUI

ISBN-10: 1466381922
EAN-13: 9781466381926

1. INTRODUCTION

Information management deals with the production, classification and communicating crucial information to internal users for efficient decision making. In a way, it deals with both accounting and non-accounting information. Therefore management accounting is a subset of information management in the sense that management accounting provides accounting information to supplement the non-accounting information provided by information management. Given the importance of information management to internal users for decision making, and to the firm for the creation of an "information capital" for better stewardship and growth, this book will examine the important issues that determine the effectiveness and efficiency of information management in ensuring an efficient, and continuous provision of information of relevance to decision making in general, and resource allocation in particular. These issues will be dealt in five chapters as follows:

Issue one to be examined in the second chapter covers the accounting foundations of information management. Information management has its foundations in the discipline of accounting, although it recognizes the potential benefits of borrowing relevant techniques from other disciplines. It expanded from its limited scope of cost accounting to a multidisciplinary integrated field aimed at assisting management in decision making. Information management includes most of the components of a conceptual framework. The chapter will present such a conceptual framework.

Issue two to be examined in the third chapter covers the behavioral foundations of information management. The type of objective function, motivations theories, heuristics, and the different models of decision making, identify the factors likely to affect the behavior and performance of an individual within the organization.

Issue three to be examined in the fourth chapter is the cognitive relativism in information management. The chapter presents a model which focuses on the cognitive processes employed by a decision maker attempting to use his/her judgment to make a decision about an information phenomenon or a business phenomenon. The model shows that judgments and decisions made about business and information phenomena are the products of a set of cognitive operations that include the observation of the information and the formation of schemata that are stored in memory and later retrieved to allow the formation of judgments and/or decisions when needed.

Issue four to be examined in the fifth chapter is the functional and data fixation that can plague the efficiency of information management. Functional fixation suggests that under certain circumstances a decision maker might be unable to adjust his or her decision process to a change in the information process that supplied him/her with input data.

Issue five is to be examined in the sixth chapter covers organizational and budgetary slack that can plague the efficiency of information management.

The book attempts to cover all these issues of relevance to the efficiency of information management by a review of the relevant literature on the subjects and the provision of possible solutions.

2. THE ACCOUNTING FOUNDATIONS OF INFORMATION MANAGEMENT

Information management is the main concern in management accounting. Management accounting is one of the areas in the field and profession of accountancy. As suggested by the 1958 American Accounting Association (AAA) Committee on Management Accounting, it "involves consideration of the ways in which accounting information may be accumulated, synthesized, analyzed, and presented in relation to specific problems, decisions, and day-to-day tasks of business management."[1] An appreciation of information management requires a good understanding of the different facets of information in organizations. A clarification of each information area will help identify the scope of information management, the possibility of an information management theory, and a taxonomy of information management techniques.

The aim of this chapter is to clarify the role of information management, and to argue for information management as a frame of reference for the justification of present and new information management.

NATURE OF ACCOUNTING

The financial community has always regarded the information discipline as one of its principal tools in the decision-making process. The primacy of decision has been stressed by both William Paton and the AAA "Statement of Basic Accounting Theory":

> The purpose of accounting may be said to that of interpreting the financial data...to provide a sound guide action by management, investor and other interested parties.[2]
>
> The committee defines accounting as the process of identifying, measuring, and communicating economic information to permit informed judgments and decisions by users of the information.[3]

Thus, accounting is perceived as utilitarian in purpose and descriptive in nature Stated in means-end terms, the end sought is good information and the means employed are descriptions. Accounting provides information for two distinct but closely related purposes: (1) reporting to managers within the organization and (2) reporting to persons outside the organization who have a legitimate interest in its affairs. More precisely the accounting system provides information for three broad objectives:

1. Internal routine reporting to managers to provide information and influence behavior regarding cost management and the planning and controlling of operations.
2. Internal nonroutine, or special, reporting to managers for strategic and tactical decisions on matters such as pricing products or services, choosing which products to emphasize or de-emphasize, investing in equipment, and formulating overall policies and long-range planning.
3. External reporting through financial statement to investors, government authorities, and other outside parties.[4]

The first two areas are those of internal or management accounting, the third is of external or financial accounting. What is the extent of the differences in scope of both financial and management accounting?

FINANCIAL VERSUS MANAGEMENT ACCOUNTING

Financial accounting deals with reporting information that pertains to the financial position, performance, and conduct of a firm for a given period to a set of users and the market in general. Management accounting is more oriented toward internal decision making and purposively channels relevant and timely information to internal managers. Both are production processes of different accounting data for different problem-solving situations.

Financial accounting is the result of applying generally accepted accounting principles (GAAP) to the recording of transactions between different entities. As such, financial accounting statements confirm to a set of rules established by the profession. Management accounting, however, reflects the use of techniques from different disciplines, including accounting, for internal problem solving. Therefore, management accounting techniques may differ from GAAP techniques and from one firm to another. They do not confirm to any set of prescribed rules, and much may be left to the decision-maker's philosophies.

In short, the frame of reference used in management accounting is much broader than that used in financial accounting. Vergil Boyd and Dale Taylor considered the specific difference to be the following:

1. The management approach places the student in the role of a *user* of financial data in decision making. The conventional approach assigns the student the role of *preparer* of financial statements for use by others.
2. The student of managerial accounting is called upon to use his or her entire knowledge of the business world in making business decisions based upon accounting data. Conventional accounting limits itself to accounting techniques, principles, and practices, and rarely deals with decisions other than those required in the preparation of financial statements.
3. An attempt is made to consider the external and internal business environment in managerial accounting.

Conventional accounting usually ignores these conditions.

4. The arrangement and managerial accounting is to make a decision related to a business problem. Conventional accounting has as its end the ability to prepare adequate financial statements.[5]

To this list of differences, it may be also added that financial accounting data are required to be objective and verifiable, while management accounting emphasizes relevance and flexibility.

MANAGEMENT VESUS COST ACCOUNTING

Although the relationship between cost accounting and management accounting has not been explicitly clarified, it is usually believed that it is one point of emphasis. Cost accounting deals mainly with cost accumulation, inventory valuation, and product costing. It emphasizes the cost side. The objective function is implicitly perceived to be cost minimization. Similarly, management accounting deals with the efficient allocation of resources.

The objective function may be perceived to be profit maximization. It is also believed that the cost accountant and the management accountant are performing different activities: cost control is in the domain of the cost accountant, while cost reduction is in the domain of the management accountant.[6] A cursory examination of accounting textbooks shows that, in general, those labeled *cost accounting* emphasize cost control while those labeled *management accounting* or *managerial accounting* emphasize planning, which may have reinforced the belief in a difference between both areas.[7] It is advisable, however, not to stress those differences, but rather to conceive of management accounting as an attempt to bring techniques from other disciplines into the area of cost accounting. In fact, in recent years, the scope of cost accounting has been enlarged in various ways:

1. It emphasizes not only the explanatory but also the predictive ability of accounting data.
2. It develops normative models to be applied in the accounting context with an emphasis on mathematical, statistical, and operations research techniques.
3. It stresses the behavioral impact of accounting information on the users.
4. It uses non accounting information—economic, environmental, and qualitative—to improve the relevance of management accounting data.
5. It merges economic and social goals and consequently draws the accountant into program budgets and "performance" auditing in not-for-profit organizations.
6. It relies on more frequent and heavier use of computers, leading to a centralization of information and the expected candidature of the management accountant for the job of the "information manager" having overall responsibility of this resource.

This enlargement of the scope of cost accounting into management accounting leads to the problem of the modern education of management accountants, which can be resolved by an exposure of students to either a proliferation of courses in the computer, quantitative, and behavioral sciences, or to an integrated multidisciplinary approach as advocated in this book. Following the same line of reasoning, the 1972 AAA Committee on Courses in Managerial Accounting made the following appropriate assumptions:

1. The role of managerial accounting encompasses the entire formalized information function of an organization.
2. The accountant is the best candidate for a manager of this information system.
3. Managerial accounting should be developed around a framework for the information-wide perspective in the analysis and design of the information function.
4. Managerial accounting should integrate material from the computer, the quantitative, and the behavior sciences areas.
5. Management accounting should continue the traditional emphasis on problems while using more sophisticated approaches to problem solving.[8]

In brief, management accounting should go beyond cost accounting and integrate various concepts from organization theory, behavioral sciences, information theory, and so on, in a multidisciplinary approach aimed at facilitating the production of information for internal decision making. In spite of these diversifications in the background of management accountants, they remain professionals, as evidenced by the growing popularity of the Certificate in Management Accounting program of the National Association of Accountants (NAA; also NA). The following excerpt from a brochure issued by the NAA highlights the new scope of the management accountant's activities:

> More and more people—inside the business world and out—realize the significant changes which have been taking place for years in accounting and the role of the accountant in business. No longer is he simply a recorder of business history. He now plays a dynamic role in making business decisions, in future planning and in almost every aspect of business operations. This new accountant is called a Management Accountant and he sits with top management because his responsibility is developing, producing and analyzing information to help management make sound decisions. Many management accountants make their way to top management positions.
>
> In response to the needs of business and at the request of many in the academic community, the National Association of Accountants has established a program to recognize professional competence in this field—a program leading to the Certificate in Management Accounting [CMA].

The CMA program requires candidates to pass a series of uniform examinations and meet specific educational and professional standards to qualify for and maintain the Certificate in Management Accounting. NA has established the Institute of Management Accounting to administer the program, conduct the examinations and grant certificates to those who qualify.

The objectives of the program are threefold:

1. to establish management accounting as a recognized profession by identifying the role of the management accountant and the underlying body of knowledge, and by outlining a course of study by which such knowledge, can be acquired;
2. to foster higher educational standards in the field of management;
3. to assist employers, educators and students by establishing objective measurement of an individual's knowledge and competence in field of management accounting.

Those management accountants are to occupy important positions in organizations and therefore have to abide by high ethical standards. Accordingly the NAA has promulgated the following ethical standards for management accountants:

Competence

Management accountants have a responsibility to:

- Maintain an appropriate level of professional competence by ongoing development of their knowledge and skills.
- Perform their professional duties in accordance with relevant laws, regulations, and technical standards.
- Prepare complete and clear reports and recommendations after appropriate analyses of relevant and reliable information.

Confidentiality

Management accountants have a responsibility to:

- Refrain from disclosing confidential information acquired in the course of their work except when authorized, unless legally obligated to do so.
- Inform subordinates as appropriate regarding the confidentiality of information acquired in the course of their work and monitor their activities to assure the maintenance of the confidentiality.

- Refrain from using or appearing to use confidential information acquired in the course of their work for unethical or illegal advantage either personally or through third parties.

Integrity

Management accountants have a responsibility to:

- Avoid actual or apparent conflicts of interest and advise all appropriate parties of any potential conflict.
- Refrain from engaging in any activity that would prejudice their ability to carry out their duties ethically.
- Refuse any gift, favor, or hospitality that would influence or would appear to influence their actions.
- Refrain from either actively or passively subverting the attainment of the organization's legitimate and ethical objectives.
- Recognize and communicate professional limitations or other constraints that would preclude responsible judgment or successful performance of an activity.
- Communicate unfavorable as well as favorable information and professional judgments or opinions.

- Refrain from engaging in or supporting any activity that would discredit the profession.

Objectivity

Management accountants have a responsibility to:

- Communicate information fairly and objectively.
- Disclose fully all relevant information that could reasonably be expected to influence an intended user's understanding of the reports, comments, and recommendations presented.[9]

MANAGEMENT ACCOUNTING THEORY

Management accounting and information management are generally understood as a process or as referring to the use of techniques. For example, the 1958 Committee on Management Accounting defines it as "the application of appropriate techniques and concepts in processing the historical and projected economic data of an entity to assist management in establishing a plan for reasonable economic objectives, and in the making of rational decisions with a view towards achieving these objectives."[10] Similarly the emergent conceptual framework of management accounting started by the National Association of accountants defines it as the process of identification, measurement, accumulation, analysis, preparation, interpretation and communication of financial information used by management to plan, evaluate, and control within an organization and to assure appropriate use of and accountability for its resources. Management accounting also comprises the preparation of financial reports for non-management groups such as shareholders, creditors, regulatory agencies, and tax authorities.[11]

Those techniques are further explicated as follows:

Identification—the recognition and evaluation of business transactions and other economic events for appropriate accounting action.

Measurement—the quantification, including estimates, of business transactions or other economic events that have occurred or may occur.

Accumulation—the disciplined and consistent approach to recording and classifying appropriate business transactions and other economic events.

Analysis—the determination of the reasons for, and the relationships of, the reported activity with other economic events and circumstances.

Preparation and Interpretation—the meaningful coordination of accounting and/or planning data to satisfy a need for information, presented in a logical format, and, if appropriate, including the conclusions drawn from those data.

Communication—the reporting of pertinent information to management and others for internal and external uses.

Plan—to gain an understanding of expected business transactions and other economic events and their impact on the organization.

Evaluate—to judge the implications of various past and/or future evnents.

Control—to ensure the integrity of financial information concerning an organization's activities or its resources.

Assure accountability—to implement the system of reporting that is closely aligned to organizational responsibilities and that contributes to the effective measurement of management performance.[12]

A generally accepted definition of a theory, as it could apply to management accounting, is that a theory represents the coherent set of hypothetical, conceptual, and pragmatic principles for a field of inquiry. Accordingly, management accounting theory may be defined as a frame of reference in the form of a set of postulates and/or principles from different disciplines by which management accounting techniques are evaluated. The task of justifying the existence of a management accounting theory lies in the definition of appropriate postulates and principles. Given the differences in the objectives between management accounting and financial accounting, the postulates of financial accounting, with some exceptions, do not hold true for management accounting. In fact, the 1961 AAA Management Accounting Committee, charged with determining the relevance of financial accounting concepts to management accounting, concluded that

1. the concepts underlying internal reporting differ in several important respects from those of external public reporting;
2. these differences are due to differences in the objectives of both areas; and
3. it is justified to develop a separate body of concepts applicable to internal reporting.[13]

There is a need, then, for the accounting profession to develop a conceptual framework in management accounting to guide the development and use of techniques. Similar to financial accounting, such a framework would include the following elements:

1. The *objectives* of management accounting as the first and important step for the development of the elements of the conceptual framework for management accounting.
2. *Qualitative characteristics* to be met as essential attributes of management accounting information.

3. *Management accounting concepts* as the foundation for the body of knowledge contained within the conceptual framework.

4. *Management accounting techniques* and procedures that constitute the internal accounting systems.

Although these elements and the total integrated framework have not yet been formalized through a deductive reasoning process, they do exist in the literature as separate attempts to resolve these issues. Each of the proposed elements of management accounting will be examined next.

OBJECTIVES OF MANAGEMENT ACCOUNTING

The objectives of management accounting are the first and essential step to the formulation of an information management theory. Then, the management accounting concepts will be true because they will be based on accepted objectives. In spite of the importance of management accounting objectives, there has never been a formal attempt by the profession to accomplish such a task. One noticeable exception, which may serve as de facto objectives of management accounting, was provided by the 1972 AAA Committee on Courses in Managerial Accounting. Four objectives were presented:

A. Management accounting should be related to the planning function of the managers. This involves:

   1. Goal identification.

2. Planning for optimal resource flows and their measurement.

B. Management accounting should be related to organizational problem areas. This includes:

1. Relating the structure of the firm to its goals.

2. Installing and maintaining an effective communication and reporting system.

3. Measuring existing resource uses, discovering exceptional performance, and identifying causal factors of such exceptions.

C. Management accounting should be related to the management control function. This includes:

Determining economic characteristics of appropriate performance areas that are significant in terms of overall goals.

Aiding to motivate desirable individual performances through a realistic communication of performance information in relation to goals.

Highlighting performance measures indicating goal incongruity within identifiable performance and responsibility areas.

D. Management accounting should be related to operating systems management, by function, product, project, or other segmentation of operations. This involves:

Measurement of relevant cost input and/or revenue or statistical measures of outputs.

Communication of appropriate data, of essentially economic character, to critical personnel on a timely basis.[14]

The NA's emerging conceptual framework defines the objectives of management accounting as well as management accountants in terms of providing information and participating in the management process. More specifically the true objectives are defined as follows:

Providing Information

Management accountants select and provide, to all levels of management, information needed for:

a. Planning, evaluating, and controlling operations;

b. Safeguarding the organization's assets; and

c. Communicating with interested parties outside the organization, such as shareholders and regulatory bodies.

Participating In the Management Process

Management accountants at appropriate levels are involved actively in the process of managing the entity. This process includes making strategic, tactical, and operating decisions and helping to coordinate the efforts of the entire organization. The management accountant participates, as part of management, in assuring that the organization operates as a unified whole in its long-run, intermediate, and short-run best interests.[15]

While these objectives reflect some of the priorities facing management accounting, they do not necessarily represent all the facets of the environment of management accounting. A formal study for the objectives of accounting is a definite must for the profession.

QUALITATIVE CHARACTERISTICS OF MANAGEMENT INFORMATION

Management information should have certain desirable properties so that benefits are achievable. The 1969 AAA Committee on Managerial Decision Models explored the application to internal reporting of the standards of relevance, verifiability, freedom from bias, and quantifiability.[16] These standards for accounting information were suggested in the AAA Statement of Basic Accounting Theory.[17] This effort was pursued by the 1974 AAA Committee on Concepts and Standards—Internal Planning and Control.[18] The Committee offered the following closely related properties as representatives of the benefits information or information systems:

1. Relevance/mutuality of objectives
2. Accuracy/precision/reliability
3. Consistency/comparability/uniformity

4. Verifiability/objectivity/neutrality/traceability

5. Aggregation

6. Flexibility/adaptability

7. Timeliness

8. Understandability/acceptability/motivation/fairness.[19]

The findings of the Committee are discussed next.

1. *Relevance/mutuality of objectives.* Relevant information is that which bears upon or is useful to "the action it is designed to facilitate or the result it is desired to produce."[20] For example, given different alternatives, the relevant costs and revenues are those expected costs and revenues that will be different for at least one of the alternatives. Historical costs may be only the basis for estimating expected future costs.

Relevance depends on the structure of the objective function. In other words, relevant information is the information on any variables in the user's objective function and must be very close to the definition implicit in the objective function. Relevance is a qualitative rather than a quantitative characteristic in the sense that information is either relevant or not.

Finally, relevance depends on the particular user receiving the information and on his or her particular decision. Some variables may be relevant to one user and not to others, and to one type of decision and not to others.

Mutuality of objectives refers to the consistency and congruency of the goals of the information users with those established by top management for the whole organization. The information provided by the internal reporting system may contribute to internal goal congruency if the signals of success or failure have the same meaning for both the total organization and its different segments. The mutuality of objectives applies also to the management accountants or the "internal information processors." Their goals should be consistent with the organizational goals.

2. *Accuracy/precision/reliability.* These properties are statistically interrelated in the sense that the notion of accuracy is statistically expressed by the concepts of precision and reliability. The specification of precision requires the specification of reliability, and vice versa.21 R. M. Cyert and H. J. Davidson define these concepts as follows: "reliability is commonly used to describe the chances that a confidence interval will contain the true value being estimated...precision is often used in describing the interval about a sample estimate."[22] While it is generally impossible to reach 100 percent accuracy, it is advisable to specify upper and lower bounds within which accuracy may be an effective property of management accounting information.

3. *Consistency/comparability/uniformity.* Consistency refers to the continued use of the same rules and procedures by the same firm over time, leading to comparability of its own statements with each other for one year to another. Uniformity refers to the use of similar rules by different firms. Consistency, uniformity, and the ensuing comparability are considered desirable criteria for financial accounting. Their relevance to management accounting differs between long-term and short-term decisions. A long-range planning decision relies on diverse, unstructured information and nonrepetitive situations, and it may be unduly hampered by an internal accounting system stressing consistency/comparability/

uniformity. However, the areas of short-run planning and performance control rely more on carefully structured information and repetitive situations, and lend themselves to an internal accounting system stressing consistency/comparability/uniformity.

4. *Verifiability/objectivity/neutrality/traceability.* Verifiability and objectivity refer to measurements that can be duplicated by independent measures using the same measurement methods. It is usually operationally measured by the dispersion of the data in terms of the variance of the data. If the measurement rules are well-specified, the verifiability of the measurement may be accomplished through a reconstruction of the initial measurement process and on the basis of evidential documents referred to as the audit trail. Traceability refers to the availability of such an audit trail. Finally, neutrality refers to the impartiality of the data in terms of its impact on different groups. A personal interest of the measurer in the data will not likely lead to neutral measurements. The degree of verifiability/objectivity/traceability of the data generated for management accounting is not as pronounced as when applied to financial accounting. However, neutrality of the information is a desirable objective, especially when the data are used for information evaluation or as a basis for distributing resources or settling claims.

5. *Aggregation.* This refers to the process of reducing the volume of data. A loss of identifiability or information is generally attributed to the process of aggregation, which may be compensated by cost savings in accounting for the information. And optimal level of aggregation is difficult to specify for either financial or management accounting. For financial accounting, the preparation of standard financial statements according to well-defined rules has led to a tendency to aggregate the information at an early stage of

information processing. For management accounting, the lack of homogeneity in the reports, the flexibility in the choice of rules for preparing these reports, and the objective to meet a variety of information needs argue in favor of a management accounting system with less aggregated data, but that takes into account the user's limitations in handling voluminous data.

6. *Flexibility/adaptability*. Flexibility refers to the degree to which data may be the basis for several types of information and reports. It depends on both the classification used for the date base into definite categories and the level of aggregation used in each of the categories. For example, purchase data may be classified under the following categories: (1) by individual product or service, (2) by individual purchaser, (3) by supplier, and so on. These data may be aggregated under the following categories: (1) by transaction, (2) by day, (3) by month, and so on.

Adaptability refers to the extent to which information derived from the data base may be tailored to, or harmonized with, the decision processes of the firm. The adaptability of an accounting system requires not only the presence of flexibility, but also an explicit process of harmonizing it with the decision process. The Committee suggested the following procedures for harmonizing:

> Such harmonizing is often accomplished iteratively through an understanding of the planning and control process, representing the latter in terms of information parameters and specifying the aggregation rules to be used in going from data base to information and analyzing the impact of such information on the planning processes. [23]

Again, given the lack of homogeneity in the management accounting reports, the large number of these reports and the desire to meet various decision needs, management accounting requires higher levels of flexibility and adaptability than financial accounting.

7. *Timeliness*. Timeliness refers to the age of the information. It has two components: interval and delay. Interval is the period of time elapsing between the preparation of two successive reports. Delay is the period of time necessary to process the data, prepare the reports, and distribute them. Timeliness is also related to the concept of real time. Wayne Boutell provides the following definition: "It [real time] refers to the time in which information is received by the particular decision maker. If the information is received in sufficient time for a decision to be made without a penalty for delay, the information is said to be received in real time."[24] Although timeliness is a uniquely desirable property of management accounting information, it is affected by cost considerations and may conflict with other criteria, such as accuracy.

8. *Understandability/acceptability/motivation/fairness.* This refers to the extent to which the user is able to use the information. Understandability refers to the ability of the user to ascertain the message transmitted. Acceptability is the recognition by the user that the problem specification and measurement criteria have been met. Fairness refers to the neutrality of the information as defined earlier. Finally, motivation refers to the attempt to secure goal congruences between the user and the organization. In brief, management accounting information should be understandable, acceptable, fire to the user, and a motivation to the user to perform in the desired manner.

MANAGEMENT INFORMATION CONCEPTS

Management information concepts based on both the objectives and qualitative characteristics of management information would constitute the basis foundation for a management information conceptual framework. Although the development and formalization of a management information conceptual framework remains to be accomplished, the literature contains references to certain identifiable management information concepts. For example, the 1972 AAA Committee on Courses in Managerial Accounting identified measurement, communication, information, system, planning, feedback, control, and cost behavior as some of the management accounting concepts "which represent a necessary, if not minimum, foundation for the body of knowledge contained within the structure."[25] Accordingly, each of these concepts will be explained next.

1. Applied to accounting, *measurement* has been defined as "an assignment of numerals to an entity's past, present, or future economic phenomena, on the basis of past or present observation and according to rules."[26] This concept is very essential to management accounting.

2. As defined by Claude Shannon and Warren Weaver, *communication* encompasses "the procedures by means of which one mechanism affects another mechanism."[27]

3. *Information* represents significant data upon which action is based. It refers to those data that reduce the uncertainty on the part of the user. Thus, data produced by management accounting should be evaluated in terms of their informational content. Although not exhaustive,

management accounting information includes the following categories:

a. financial information resulting from the flow of financial resources within the organization,
b. production information resulting from the physical flow of resources within the organization,
c. personnel information resulting from the flow of people within the organization, and
d. marketing information resulting from the interaction with the market for the organization's products.

4. *System* refers to an entity consisting of two or more interacting components or subsystems intended to achieve a goal. Management accounting is generally a subsystem of the accounting information system, which is itself a subsystem of the total management information system within the organization. The interaction of the management accounting system with all the other systems within the organization, and especially the integration of all these systems, is essential for an efficient functioning of the organization. A management accounting system may be defined as *the set of human and capital resources within an organization that is responsible for the production and dissemination of information deemed relevant for internal decision making.*

5. *Planning* refers to the management function of setting objectives, establishing policies, and choosing means of accomplishment. Planning may be practiced at different levels in the organization, from strategic to operational, and may have behavioral implications.

6. *Feedback* refers to the output of a process that returns to become an input to the process in order to initiate control. It is basically a revision of the planning process to accommodate new environmental events.

7. *Control* refers to monitoring and evaluating of performance to determine the degree of conformance of actions to plans. Ideally, planning precedes control, which is followed by a feedback corrective action or a feedforward preventive action.

8. *Cost Behavior*: cost results from the use of an asset for the generation of revenues. The identification, classification, and estimation of costs is essential to any evaluation of courses of action.

Although not exhaustive, this list represents concepts that are representative of those foundation components essential to a grasp of the management accounting process. This is very much in line with the NA's definition of the responsibilities of a management accountant:

1. *Planning.* Quantifying and interpreting the effects on the organization of planned transactions and other economic events. The planning responsibility, which includes

strategic, tactical, and operating aspects, requires that the accountant provide quantitative historical and prospective information to facilitate planning. It includes participation in developing the planning system, setting obtainable goals, and choosing appropriate means of monitoring the progress toward the goals

2. *Evaluating.* Judging implications of historical and expected events and helping to choose the optimum course of action. Evaluating includes translating date into trends and relationships. Management accountants must communicate effectively and promptly the conclusions derived from the analyses.

3. *Controlling.* Assuring the integrity of financial information concerning an organization's activities and resources; monitoring and measuring performance and inducing any corrective actions required to return the activity to its intended course. Management accountant provide information to executives operating in functional areas who can make use of it to achieve desirable performance.

4. *Assuring accountability of resources.* Implementing a system of reporting that is aligned with organizational responsibilities. This reporting system will contribute to the effective use of resources and measurement of management performance. The transmission of management's goals and objective throughout the organization in the form of assigned responsibilities is a basis for identifying accountability. Management accountants muse provide an accounting and reporting system that will accumulate and report appropriate

revenues, expenses, assets, liabilities, and related quantitative information to managers. Managers then will have better control over these elements.

5. *External reporting.* Preparing financial reports based on generally accepted accounting principles, or other appropriate bases, for non management groups such as shareholders, creditors, regulatory agencies, and tax authorities. Management accountants should participate in the process of developing the accounting principles that underline external reporting.[28]

MANAGEMENT INFORMATION TECHNIQUES

Management information techniques should be derived and supported by the management information conceptual framework. Given the absence of such a framework, there is no consensus on a list of management information techniques. Most management information textbooks include standard cost accounting techniques and only a few attempts at introducing behavioral and/or quantitative considerations in separate chapters. What is needed is a structure that will allow an integration of accounting, organizational, behavioral, quantitative, and other techniques of relevance to internal decision making. The AAA Report of the Committee on Courses in Managerial Accounting proposes such a structure:

Introductory Material

Systems theory and accounting

Communications, measurement, and information concepts

Criteria development

Feedback and control mechanisms

Information systems

Accounting for management planning and control

Cost concepts and techniques

Cost Determination for Assets

Job order and process costing

Standard costing system

Direct versus absorption costing

By-product and joint product costing

Cost allocation practices

Accounting for human resources

Planning

Strategic planning

Continuous planning

Investment decisions

Comprehensive budgets

Cost-volume-profit analysis

Problems of alternative choice

Management Control

Responsibility accounting

Cost centers

Financial performance centers

Investment centers

Centralized versus decentralized structures

Concern for goal congruence

Transfer pricing

Evaluation methods

Performance reporting

Operational Control

Internal control

Project control

Inventory control[29]

Although not exhaustive, this list represents most of the techniques included in management information textbooks, but still fails to incorporate behavioral, organization, and decisional models essential to an adequate performance of a management information system of knowledge known as management accounting.

There is, however, no consensus on what the cost/managerial curriculum content should be, as evidenced by Exhibit 2.1. This is particularly due to the absence of a conceptual framework for management accounting. In addition, there is no consensus on what are the appropriate techniques for each of the management accounting topics included. W. B. Polland used the following overhead variance analysis problem to illustrate the varieties of treatment existing in management accounting:[30]

Problem: the following information is available:

Budgeted production		9,000 units
Actual production		9,450 units
Standard DIRECT LABOR HOURS (DLHs) per unit		3
Actual DLHs (total)		28,000
Standard DLHs (total)	(9450 * 3)	28,350
Actual FIXED OVERHEAD (FOH)		$56,700
Actual VARIABLE OVERHEAD (VOH)		$54,000
FOH Rate (per DLH)		$2
VOH Rate (per DLH)		$1

The partial analysis of the overhead variance is shown in Exhibit 2.2. The variety of treatments used in the major textbooks of the times is illustrated in Exhibit 1.3.

There is a very useful framework for relating management accounting topics. The framework, proposed by Professor Larry N. Bitner, is shown in Exhibit 1.4.[31] The framework makes three important distinctions :

Exhibit 2.1

A Summary of Prior Studies of Cost/Managerial Curriculum Content (ranked lists of topics—maximum of 20 topics displayed)

Deakin and Summers (1975)	*Knight and Zook (1982)*	*Lander and Reinstein (1987)*	*Robinson and Barrett (1988)*	*VanZante (1988)*
Performance Evaluation	Preparation of Principal Statements	Internal Control and Accounting Systems	Job Order Costing	Cost Behavior
Responsibility Accounting	CVP Relationships	Operational Budgeting	CVP Relationships	Computer Systems
Internal Control	Current Asset Valuation	Standard Costs	Full Absorption Costing	Forecasting
Tax Factors in Business Decisions	Liabilities Valuation	Capital Budgeting	Variable Costing	Financial Statement Analysis
Profit Planning	Long-term Asset Valuation	Product Costing	Standard Costs	Variance Analysis
Cash Management	Equity Valuation	Cost Behavior and Variances	Process Costing	Working Capital Management
Organization Theory	Other Assets Valuation	Organizational Behavior	Flexible Budgets	Financial Statement Preparation

Information Systems Design	Cost Accumulation Systems	Cost Accumulation, General Accounting, Taxes	Direct Costing	Capital Budgeting
Internal Reporting	Cost Control, Flexible Budgets, Standards	Inventories	Joint Costs	Information Content
Forecasting	Short-term Budgeting	Segments and Decentralization	Budgeted Financial Statements	Segment Accounting
Accounting Principles Impact	Ratio Analysis	Economics and Government	Short-term Planning	Valuation Bases
Behavioral Implications	Disclosure Standards and Procedures	Quantitative Methods	Spoilage, Waste, Scrap	Ethical Considerations
Capital Budgeting	Internal Control	Cost Allocation	Responsibility Accounting	Long-term Financing
Systems Implementation	Working Capital Management	(Results summarized in these 13 categories)	Capital Budgeting	Motivation and Perception
Internal and Managerial Auditing	Long-term Financing		Return on Investment	Tax Regulations
Information Systems Administration	Long-run Forecasting and Planning		Common Costs in Performance Evaluation	Behavioral Implications

Divisional Reporting	Capital Budgeting	Overhead Control	Internal Audits
Information Economics	Mergers and Acquisitions	Divisional Performance	Microeconomic Theory
Computer Use in Decision-Making	Divisional Performance and Transfer Pricing	Transfer Pricing	Regulatory Bodies
Nonfinancial Measures of Performance	SEC	Residual Income	Organizational Theory

Source: Reprinted with permission from *Journal of Accounting Education* (Fall): 210-211, A. M. Novin, M. A. Pearson, and S. V. Senge, "Improving the Curriculum for Aspiring Management Accountants: The Practitioner's Point of View," copyright 1990, Pergamon Press pls.

Exhibit 2.2

Partial Analysis of Overhead Variances

VARIABLE OVERHEAD:

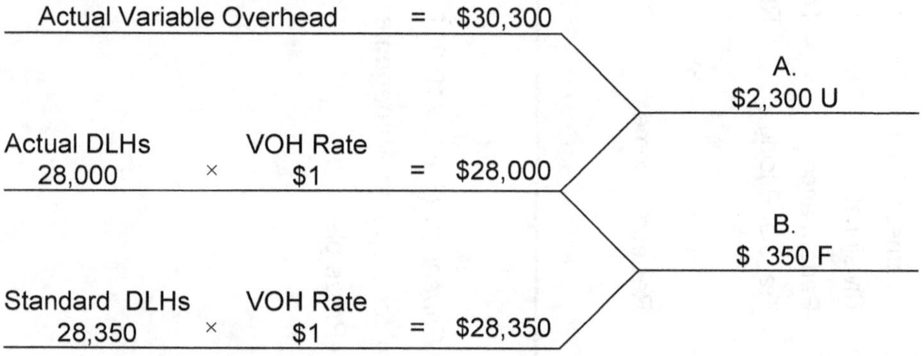

VARIABLE OVERHEAD:

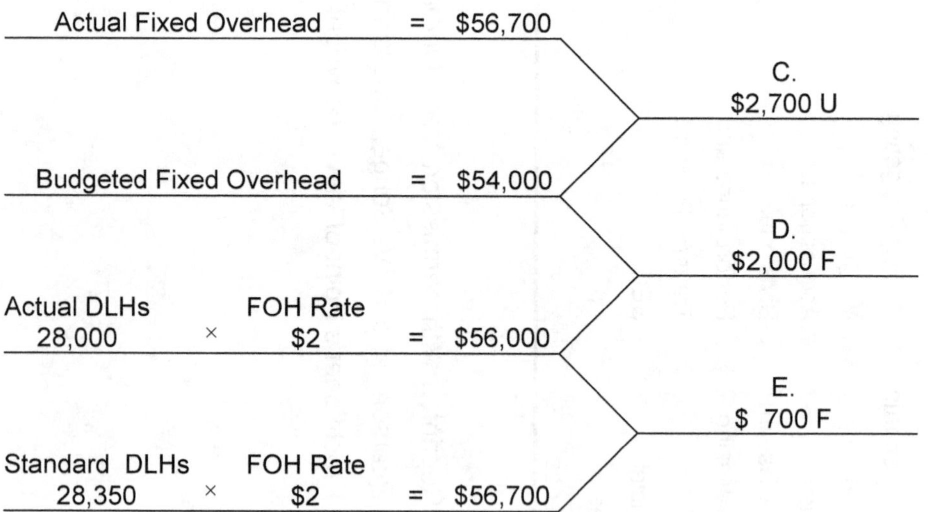

Exhibit 2.3

Overhead Variance Analysis—Comparison

ASCH [1983]	BELKAOUI [1983] Model A	BELKAOUI [1983] Model B	BROCK and PALMER [1984]	CASHIN and POLIMENI [1981]	CHATFIELD and NEILSON [1983]
TWO-WAY	**TWO-WAY**	**TWO-WAY**	**TWO-WAY**	**TWO-WAY**	**TWO-WAY**
1. None	Price A+C+D	ControllableA+B+C	OH Budget A+B+C	Controllable A+B+C	OH Budget A+B+C
2. None	Efficiency B+E	Uncontrollable D+E	OH Volume D+E	Volume D+E	FOH Volume D+E
THREE -WAY	***THREE -WAY***	**THREE -WAY**	**THREE –WAY**	**THREE -WAY**	**THREE -WAY**
1. None	Spending A+ C	Spending A+ C	Spending A+ C	Spending A+C	Combined OH Spending A+C
2. None	Efficiency B+E	Efficiency B	Efficiency B	Efficiency B+E	VOH Efficiency B
3. None	Idle Capacity D	Idle Capacity D+E	OH Volume D+E	Idle Capacity D	FOH Volume D+E

FOUR-WAY	***FOUR-WAY***	**FOUR-WAY**	**FOUR-WAY**	**FOUR-WAY**
1. VOH Expenditure A	Spending A +C	None	Spending A+C	VOH Spending A
2. VOH Efficiency B	VOH Efficiency B	None	VOH Efficiency B	VOH Efficiency B
3. FOH Expenditure C	Idle Capacity D	None	Idle Capacity D	FOH Spending C
4. FOH Volume D+E	FOH Efficiency E	None	FOH Efficiency E	FOH Volume D+E

Exhibit 2.3 (continued)

KILLOUGH and LEININGER [1984]	**LOUDERBACK and HIRSCH [1982]**	**MATZ and USRY [1984]**	**MORIARITY and ALLEN [1984]**	**MORSE [1981]**
TWO-WAY	**TWO-WAY**	**TWO-WAY**	**TWO-WAY**	**TWO-WAY**
1. Controllable A+B+C 2. Volume D+E	None None	Controllable A+B+C Volume D+E	None None	OH Budget A+B+C OH Volume D+E
THREE -WAY	THREE –WAY	**THREE -WAY**	**THREE -WAY**	**THREE -WAY**
1. Spending A+C 2. Efficiency B 3. Volume D+E	Spending A+C Efficiency B Application D+E	Spending A+C Efficiency B+E Idle Capacity D	Combined Price A+C VOH Quantity B Volume (Denominator) D+E	OH Spending A+C OH Efficiency B OH Volume D+E
FOUR-WAY	FOUR-WAY	FOUR-WAY	**FOUR-WAY**	**FOUR-WAY**
1. VOH Spending A 2. Efficiency B 3. FOH Spending C 4. Volume D+E	VOH Price A VOH Efficiency B FOH Budget C FOH Application D+E	Spending A+C VOH Efficiency B Idle Capacity D FOH Efficiency E	VOH Price A VOH Quantity B FOH Price C Volume (Denominator) D+E	VOH Spending A VOH Efficiency B FOH Budget C FOH Volume D+E

Exhibit 2.3 (continued)

DEAKIN and MAHER [1984]	**DOPUCH, BIRNBERG and DEMSKI [1982]**	**GRAY and RICKETTS [1983]**	**HARTLEY [1983]**	**HORNGREN [1982]**
TWO-WAY	**TWO-WAY**	**TWO-WAY**	**TWO-WAY**	**TWO-WAY**
1. None 2. None	None None	Budget A+B+C Volume D+E	Controllable A+B+C Noncontrollable D+E	Flexible Budget A+B+C Production Volume D+E
THREE -WAY	THREE -WAY	**THREE -WAY**	**THREE -WAY**	**THREE -WAY**
1. None 2. None 3. None	Price A+C Quantity B Volume D+E	Spending A+C Efficiency B Volume D+E	Spending A+C Efficiency B Noncontrollable D+E	Price (Spending) A+C Efficiency B Production Volume D+E
FOUR-WAY	FOUR-WAY	FOUR-WAY	**FOUR-WAY**	**FOUR-WAY**
1. VOH Price A 2. Efficiency B 3. FOH Price C 4. Production Volume D+E	None None None None	None None None None	VOH Spending A VOH Efficiency B FOH Spending C Noncontrollable D+E	Price (Spending) A Efficiency B Budget C Production Volume D+E

Exhibit 2.3 (continued)

MOST and LEWIS [1982]	**RAYBURN [1983]**	**SCHMIEDICKE and NAGY [1983]**	**SHILLINGLAW [1982]**	**WALKER [1982]**
TWO-WAY	**TWO-WAY**	**TWO-WAY**	**TWO-WAY**	**TWO-WAY**
1. Spending A+B+C 2. Volume D+E	Controllable A+B+C Volume D+E	Budget A+B+C Volume D+E	Spending A+B+C Volume D+E	None None
THREE -WAY	THREE –WAY	**THREE -WAY**	**THREE -WAY**	**THREE -WAY**
1. Spending A+C 2. Efficiency B+E 3. Volume D	OH Spending A+C VOH Efficiency B Volume D+E	Budget (Spending)A+C Efficiency B+E Capacity D	Spending A+C Labor Efficiency B Volume D+E	None None None
FOUR-WAY	FOUR-WAY	FOUR-WAY	**FOUR-WAY**	**FOUR-WAY**
1. None 2. None 3. None 4. None	VOH Spending A VOH Efficiency B FOH Spending C Volume D+E	None None None None	None None None None	VOH Expenditure A VOH Efficiency B FOH Expenditure C FOH Volume D+E

Source: Reprinted with permission from *Journal of Accounting Education* (Spring): 214-217, W. B. Pollard, "Teaching Standard Costs: A Look at Textbook Differences in Overhead Variance Analysis," Copyright 1986, Pergamon Press plc.

Exhibit 2.4

Revised Framework for Relating Management Accounting Topics

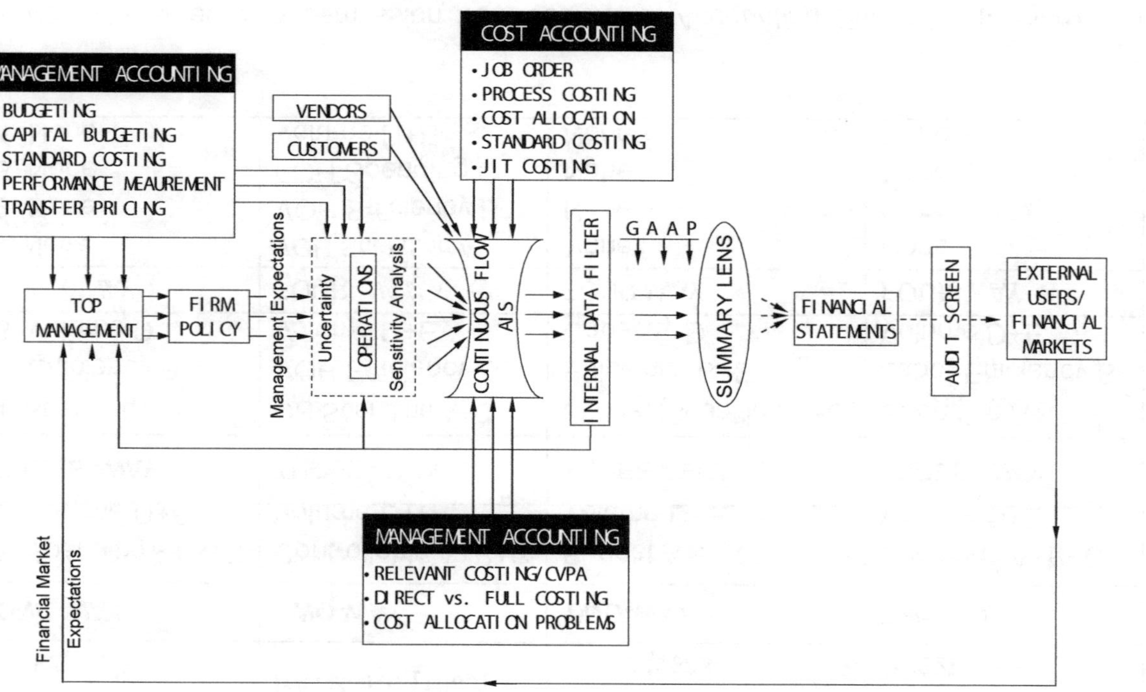

Source: Larry N. Bitner, "A Framework for Teaching Management Accounting," *Issues in Accounting Education* (Spring 1991): 118. Reprinted with permission.

Exhibit 2.5

Tentative Management Accounting Conceptual Framework

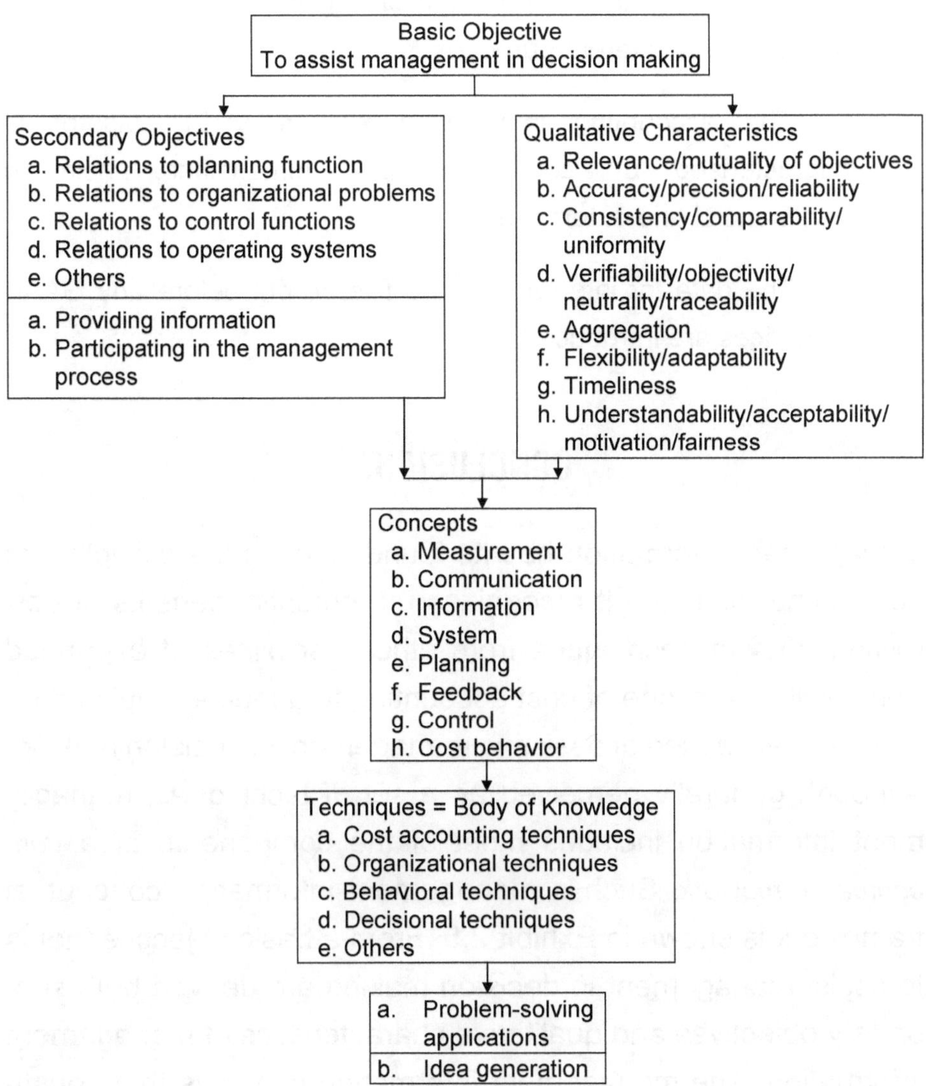

1. Management and cost accounting topics are differentiated following R. N. Anthony's distinctions between the themes of the two subdisciplines: the primary theme of cost accounting is to measure full cost while the pricing theme of management accounting is different purposes.[32]

2. The accounting information system (AIS) pulsator is characterized by continuous flow dimensions, including nonfinancial and external data.

3. The data for internal use are filtered out before any GAAP influences are introduced.

CONCLUSIONS

Management information has its foundations in the discipline of accounting, although it recognizes the potential benefits of borrowing relevant techniques from other disciplines. It expanded from its limited scope of cost accounting to a multi-disciplined integrated field aimed at assisting management in decision making. Although generally perceived as a set of techniques, management information includes most of the components of a *conceptual framework.* Such a management information conceptual framework is shown in Exhibit 2.5. From a basic objective that is to assist management in decision making are derived both secondary objectives and qualitative characteristics of management information. The management information concepts that constitute the foundation components essential to an understanding of the management information techniques or body of knowledge rest on their conformance to both the objectives and qualitative characteristics of management information.

. Because of the lack of consensus on these components, the conceptual framework presented in Exhibit 2.5 is only tentative before a formalization by the information management profession. What must be retained from this exercise is that *management accounting, and management information are, first, an accounting subsystem and, second, may be fit in an "emerging" theoretical structure.*

NOTES

1. American Accounting Association (AAA), Committee on Management Accounting, "Report of the 1958 Committee on Management Accounting," *The Accounting Review* (April 1959): 210.

2. William Paton, *Essentials of Accounting* (New York: Macmillan 1949), p.2.

3. American Accounting Association, *A Statement of Basic Accounting Theory* (Evanston, Ill.: American Accounting Association, 1966), p.1.

4. C. T. Horngren and G. Foster, *Cost Accounting: A Managerial Emphasis,* 7th ed. (Englewood Cliffs, NJ: Prentice-Hall, 1991).

5. Vergil Boyd and Dale Taylor, "The Magic Words—Managerial Accounting," *The Accounting Review* (January 1961): 210.

6. R. G. Bassett, "Management Accounting Defined," *The Cost Accountant* (October 1962): 386.

7. James S. Earley, "Recent Developments in Cost Accounting and the Marginal Analysis," *The Journal of Political Economy* (June 1955): 299.

8. AAA Committee on Courses in Managerial Accounting, “Report of the Committee on Courses in Managerial Accounting,” *The Accounting Review,* Supplement to Vol. 47 (1972): 2.

9. National Association of Accountants; *Standards of Ethical Conduct for Management Accountants* (New York: NA, June 1, 1983), pp. 1-2.

10. AAA Committee on Management Accounting, “Report of the 1958 Committee on Management Accounting,” p. 210.

11. National Association of Accountants, *Definition of Management Accounting,* Statement Number 1A (New York: NA, March 18, 1981), p. 4.

12. Ibid, pp. 4-5.

13. AAA 1961 Committee on Management Accounting, “Report of the Management Accounting Committee,” *The Accounting Review* (July 1962).

14. AAA Committee on Courses in Managerial Accounting, “Report of the Committee on Courses in Managerial Accounting,” pp. 6-7.

15. National Association of Accountants (NAA; NA), *Objectives of Management Accounting, Statement on Management Accounting 1B* (NA, June 17, 1988), p. 2.

16. AAA Committee on Managerial Decision Models, “Report of the Committee on Managerial Decision Models,” *The Accounting Review,* Supplement to Vol. 44 (1969): 47-58.

17. AAA, *Accounting Theory,* pp. 51-55.

18. AAA Committee on Concepts and Standards—Internal Planning and Control, “Report of the Committee on Concepts and Standards—

Internal Planning and Control," *The Accounting Review,* Supplement to Vol. 49 (1974): 83.

19. Ibid., p. 83.

20. AAA, *Accounting Theory,* p. 9.

21. Richard M. Cyert and H. Justin Davidson, *Statistical Sampling for Accounting Information* (Englewood Cliffs, NJ: Prentice-Hall, 1962), p. 49.

22. Ibid.

23. AAA Committee on Concepts and Standards—Internal Planning and Control, "Report," p. 91.

24. Wayne S. Boutell, *Computer Oriented Business Systems* (New York: Prentice-Hall, 1968), p. 152.

25. AAA Committee on Concepts and Standards—Internal Planning and Control, "Report," p. 91.

26. AAA Committee on Foundations of Accounting Measurement, "Report of the Committee on Foundations of Accounting Measurement," *The Accounting Review,* Supplement to Vol. 46 (1971): 3.

27. Claude E. Shannon and Warren Weaver, *The Mathematical Theory of Communication* (Urbana, Ill.: University of Illinois Press, 1949), p. 95.

28. NAA, *Objectives of Management Accounting,* pp. 3-4.

29. AAA Committee on Courses in Managerial Accounting, "Report on Courses in Managerial Accounting," pp. 9-10.

30. W. B. Pollard, "Teaching Standard Costs: A Look at Textbook Differences in Overhead Variance Analysis," *Journal of Accounting*

Education (Spring 1986): 212.

31. Larry N. Bitner, "A Framework for Teaching Management Accounting," *Issues in Accounting Education* (Spring 1991): 112-119.

32. R. N. Anthony, "Reminiscences About Management Accounting," *Journal of Management Accounting Research* (Fall 1989): 1-20.

REFERENCES

American Accounting Association. Committee on Courses in Managerial Accounting. "Report of the Committee on Coursed in Managerial Accounting." *The Accounting Review*, Supplement to Vol. 47 (1972): 1-14.

———. Committee on the Future Structure, Content, and Scope of Accounting Education. "Future Accounting Education: Preparing for the Expanding Profession." *Issues in Accounting Education*, (Spring 1986): 168-195.

———. Committee on Management Accounting. "Report of the 1958 Committee on Management Accounting." *The Accounting Review* (April 1959).

———. Committee on Managerial Decision Models. "Report of the Committee on Managerial Decision Models." *The Accounting Review*, Supplement to Vol. 44 (1969): 43-77.

Boyd, Vergil, and Taylor, Dale. "The Magic Words—Managerial Accounting." *The Accounting Review* (January 1961): 105-111.

Bruns, W. J. Jr., and Kaplan, R. S. *Accounting and Management: Field Study Perspectives.* Boston: Harvard Business School Press, 1987.

Corman, E. J. "A Writing Program for Accounting Courses." *Journal of Accounting Education* (Fall 1986): 85-95.

Crossman, Paul T. "The Nature of Management Accounting." *The Accounting Review* (April 1958): 222-227.

Davidson, H. Justin, and Trueblood, Robert M. "Accounting for Decision Making." *The Accounting Review* (October 1961): 577-582.

Deakin, E. B., and Summers, E. J. "A Survey of Curriculum Topics Relevant to the Practice of Management Accounting." *The Accounting Review* (April 1975): 380-383.

DeMaris, E. J., and Copeland, B. K. "The Critical Need for Educational Standards in Management Accounting." *Corporate Accounting* (Winter 1984): 47-53.

Donbrovski, Willis J. "Managerial Accounting: A Frame of Reference." *Management Accounting* (August 1965).

Firmin, Peter A., and Linn, James J. "Information Systems and Managerial Accounting." *The Accounting Review* (January 1968): 75-82.

Godfrey, James T., and Prince, Thomas R. "The Accounting Model from an Information Systems Perspective." *The Accounting Review* (January 1971): 75-89.

Hirsch, M. L., and Collins, J. D. "An Integrated Approach to Communication Skills in an Accounting Curriculum." *Journal of Accounting Education* (Spring 1988): 15-31.

Johnson, h. T., and Kaplan, R. S. *Relevance Lost: The Rise and Fall of Management Accounting.* Boston: Harvard Business School Press, 1987.

Killough, Larry N. "Does Management Accounting Have a Theoretical Structure?" *Management Accounting* (April 1972).

Kircher, Paul. “Theory and Research in Management Accounting.” *The Accounting Review* (January 1961): 43-45.

Knight, R. E. and Zook, D. R. “Controllers and CPAs Evaluate the Relevance of Educational Topics.” *Management Accounting* (November 1982): 30-34.

Lander, G. R., and Reinstein, A. “Identifying a Common Body of Knowledge for Management Accounting.” *Issues in Accounting Education* (Fall 1987): 264-280.

May, G. S., and Arevalo, C. “Integrating Effective Writing Skills in the Accounting Curriculum.” *Journal of Accounting Education* (Spring 1983): 119-126.

Parks, S. B. “Bridging the Gap.” *Management Accounting* (March 1987): 56.

Polland, W. B. “The Teaching Standard Costs: A Look at Textbook Differences in Overhead Variance Analysis.” *Journal of Accounting Education* (Spring 1986): 211-220.

Porter, G. L., and Akers, M. D. “In Defense of Management Accounting.” *Management Accounting* (November 1987): 58-62.

Reider, B., and Saunders, G. “Management Accounting Education: A Defense of Criticisms.” *Accounting Horizons* (December 1988): 58-62.

Robinson, M. A., and Barrett, M. E. “The Content of Management Accounting Curricula.” *The Accounting Educators’ Journal* (Spring 1988): 49-60.

Senge, S. V. "The CPA in Industry: Meeting the Relevance Challenge." *The Ohio CPA Journal* (Autumn 1987): 5-10.

Shenkin, William G., Welsh, A., and Bear, James A., Jr. "Thomas Jefferson Management Accountant." *The Journal of Accountancy* (April 1972).

Singer, Frank A. "Management Accounting." *The Accounting Review* (January 1961): 112-118.

3. THE BEHAVIORAL FOUNDATIONS

Information management is built on behavioral foundations. Its explicit aim is to affect the behavior of individuals in a desirable direction. To accomplish this purpose, information management has to be adapted to the different characteristics that shape the "cognitive make-up" of individuals within an organization and affect their performance. In general, these characteristics pertain to three factors: (1) the perception by the individual of what should be the objective function or goals in the firm; (2) the various factors likely to motivate the individual to perform; and (3) the decision-making model most relevant to particular contexts and most preferred by the individual. Although these factors do not constitute an individual within an organization, they have been identified in the literature of various disciplines as essential factors to be considered for an understanding of an individual behavior within an organization and the design of any information system.

Thus, information management requires a good grasp of the behavioral concepts; namely, the objective function in management accounting, motivation theories, and models of decision making. Each of these concepts identifies factors and situations that influence the individual behavior and indicates avenues for information management to adapt its services.

THE OBJECTIVE FUNCTION IN INFORMATION MANAGEMENT

Many authors in the field of complex organizations define an organization as a social system that is created to achieve certain specific goals or objectives. For example, Amitai Etzioni defines organizations as "social units (or human groupings) deliberately constructed and reconstructed to seek specific goals."1 Richard Hall states:

> An organization is a collectivity with a relatively identifiable boundary, a normative order, authority ranks, community systems, and membership coordinating systems; this collectivity exists on a relatively continuous basis in an environment and engages in activities that are usually related to a goal or a set of goals.[2]

The concept of organizational goal and/or objective has not, however, been clearly defined in the literature. The general goals refer to the intentions or wishes espoused by those persons who develop them. For example, V. Buck gives the following operational definition of organizational goals:

It is the decision to commit resources for certain activities and to withhold them from certain others that operationally defines the organization's goals. Verbal pronouncements are insufficient for defining goals; the speaker must put his resources where his mouth is if something is to be considered a goal.[3]

Different typologies of goals have also been proposed. First, j. D. Thompson differentiated between goals held for an organization and goals of an organization.[4] The former are held by persons who are not members of the organization but have a given interest in the activities of the firm, such as clientele, investors, action groups, and so on. The latter are held by persons who are part of the "dominant coalition" in terms of holding enough control to commit the organization to a given direction.

C. Perrow made a distinction between "official goals" and "operative goals."[5] Official goals refer to those objectives or general purposes stated either orally or in writing by key members. Operative goals refer to the designated objectives based on the actual operating policies of the organization. Etzioni refers to such goals as real goals. They constitute "the future states toward which a majority of the organizational means and major organizational commitments ...are directed, and which, in cases of conflict with goals which are stated but command few resources, have clear priority."[6]

Each discipline conceives a different goal or objective in its examination of profit-oriented organizations. The discipline of economics, for example, in its neoclassical approach views profit maximization as the single determinant of behavior. As seen in a previous chapter, organizational and management theories have provided various behavioral theories of the firm. In information management, as in corporate finance, neither the economic model nor the behavioral model appears entirely suitable. In fact, both models have influenced three held views of business behavior applicable to information management: the shareholder wealth maximization model, the managerial welfare maximization model, and the social welfare maximization model.[7] Each of these models constitutes an acceptable objective of profit-oriented organizations in the field of management accounting. Because the scope and practice of management accounting is heavily influenced by these assumptions, each of them will be examined next.

The Shareholder Wealth Maximization Model

In most textbooks in the field of corporate finance and specifically in information management, authors operate on the assumption that management's primary goal is to maximize the wealth of its stockholders. This view is referred to as the shareholder wealth maximization (SWM) model. According to this model, the firm accepts all projects yielding more than the cost of capital, and in equity financing prefers retaining earnings to issuing new stocks. It also assumes that earnings are objectively determined to show the true financial position of the firm to its owners and other users. In fact, the SWM model translates into maximizing the price of the common stock. Management is assumed to use decision rules and techniques that are in the best interests of the stockholders. In a management accounting context, SWM implies an acceptance by management of budgeting and control standards, a rejection of slack budgeting, any suboptimizing behavior, and an adoption of management accounting techniques that are in the best interests of the owners of the firm. If management behaves otherwise, its right to mange may be either questioned or revoked, given that stockholders own the firm and elect the management team. E. Solomon made a similar suggestion as follows:

But what if management has other motives, such as maximizing sales or size, growth or market share, or their own survival, or peace of mind? These operating goals do not necessarily conflict with the operating goal of wealth maximization. Indeed, a good case could be made for the thesis that wealth maximization also maximizes the achievement of these other objectives. But the point of issue is what if there is a conflict? What, for example, if management's quest for its own peace of mind or for some other goal consistently leads it to reject operating decisions that should be accepted by the wealth-maximizing criterion? The traditional answer is that such a management will be replaced sooner or later, and this is the only answer possible. Legally, management governs only as the appointed representatives of the owners. It may reject over-all goals so long as it substitutes goals which are designed to promote that of society as a whole. But if it rejects owner-oriented goals and socially-oriented goals in favor of goals that are solely management-oriented and which lead to substantially different courses of action, its right to govern is open to question.[8]

The Managerial Welfare Maximization Model

Another school of thought maintains that a different objective function other than shareholder wealth maximization exists for the firm—namely, that managers run firms for their own benefits. It is maintained that because the stock of most large firms is widely held, the managers of such firms have a great deal of freedom. This being in the case, they may be tempted for personal benefits to pursue an objective other than shareholder welfare maximization. This school of thought is generally referred to as the managerial welfare maximization (MWM) model. So rather than maximizing profits, the managers may maximize sales or assets,[9] the rate of growth,[10] or managerial utility.[11] As a consequence, managers may engage in suboptimization schemes as long as they contribute to their own welfare. For example, an entrenched management may avoid risky ventures even though the returns to stockholders would be high enough to justify the endeavor. In a management accounting context, MWM implies a lesser acceptance by management of budgeting and control standards, a resource to slack budgeting and any suboptimization behavior, a manipulation or avoidance within legality of full disclosure in order to present the firm's operation favorably (i.e., income smoothing), and, finally, adoption of management accounting techniques that are in the best interest of managers. In a recent survey, B. Branch concludes as follows:

The evidence to date may be summarized as follows. Many managers have considerable discretion to substitute their own interests for that of the stockholders. Stockholder and manager interests can conflict or be independent in significant respects. The extent to which firms are managed in stockholder interests vary considerably. Most of the empirical work suggests that firm managed in stockholders' interests tend in some sense to outperform management-oriented firms.[12]

That managers may elect to substitute their own different interests raises the question of how goals within MWM are "determined" or "set" in decisions to commit the organization to a particular course of action. Three distinct models have been identified to represent the goal-setting processes: the bargaining model, the problem-solving model, and the coalition model.[13] Because they present good conceptualizations of the goal determination process under MWM, they are briefly presented next.[14]

The Bargaining Model. The bargaining model depicts goal determination as the result of an open-minded negotiation process among all interested parties leading to a series of trade-offs and compromises. It is based on three important assumptions:

1. There is an active group of participants (internal or external) who impose demands on the organization.
2. These demands are conflicting; they cannot be accommodated simultaneously.
3. The individuals or groups are interdependent.[15]

The Problem-Solving Model. The problem-solving model describes goal determination as the result of successive decisions made by high level administrators. It is based on three important assumptions:

1. Policy commitments are made within a set of constraints or requirements that are known to decision makers.

2. These constraints can be ranked and a preferred set accommodated.
3. The goals of different individuals or groups can be simultaneously satisfied.[16]

The Dominant Coalition Model. Given the existence of controlling interests in the firm, the dominant coalition model describes goal determination as the result of decisions made by those who control the ends of which policies and resources are committed. It is based on two assumptions:

1. There are many persons or groups who hold goals for an organization. These goals are frequently in conflict and cannot all be accommodated.
2. One individual or group does not have sufficient power alone to act unilaterally. Power is dispersed. Collective behavior is required to secure support for goals.[17]

The Social Welfare Maximization Model

The climate in which businesses operate is changing with pressures on organizations to be more sensitive to the impact of behavior on society. In adopting a more socially responsible attitude and responding to the pressures of new dimensions—social, human, and environmental—organizations may have to alter their main objective, whether SWM or MWM, to include as an additional constraint the welfare of society at large. This view may be referred to as the social welfare maximization (SOWM) model. Under SOWM, the firm undertakes all projects that, in addition to the usual profitability objective, minimize the social costs and maximize social benefits created by the productive operations of the firm. Thus, under SOWM the firm is not only liable to the shareholders and managers, but also to the society at large. Given the different interest groups in the society at large, the organization may have to develop different corporate purposes. For example, it was reported that one group has defined eight corporate purposes: "profit, sensitivity to natural and human environment, growth responsiveness to consumer needs, equitable distributions of benefits, dynamic business structure, fair treatment of employees, and legal and ethical behavior."[18]

In an information management context, SOWM implies the developing of a social reporting system oriented toward the measurement of social performance, including not only social costs but also social benefits. It suggests the development of a new concept of organization performance that will be more indicative of the firm's social responsibility than is provided by conventional accounting. For example, the AAA Committee on Measurement of Social Cost suggested a total organization performance, which is a function of "five outputs.":

1. Net income, which benefits stockholders and provides resources for further usiness growth
2. Human resource contribution, which assists the individual in the organization to develop new knowledge or skills

3. Public contribution, which helps the organization's community to function and provides services for its constituency

4. Environmental contribution (closely allied with public contribution), which affects "quality of life" for society

5. Product or service contribution, which affects customer well-being and satisfaction[19]

While a theory of social accounting is still emerging in the new public interest accounting paradigm, the proposed objectives and concepts for social accounting shown in Exhibit 2.1 offer an interesting beginning.

However, regardless of the objective function adopted by managers, social reporting and particularly social reports are needed by management for relevant decision making and to comply with both social pressures and legal requirements.

MOTIVATION THEORIES

Motivation is related to the intrinsic forces within the individual—namely, the motives and unsatisfied needs of the individual. More explicitly, motivation is concerned with "how behavior gets started, is energized, is sustained, is directed, is stopped, and what kind of subjective reaction is presented in the organization while all this is going on."[20] For this reason, motivation is important for an organization and for information management.

It basically refers to an individual's needs or motives that make that individual act in a specific manner. It relates all aspects of individual behavior where a deliberate and conscious action is initiated in the organization to direct individuals so that they can satisfy their needs as much as possible while they strive to accomplish the objectives of the organization. These actions may be initiated either directly by the managers' actions or through the adoption of appropriate information management techniques. Thus, information management techniques necessitate a good grasp of motivation in organizations. The identification of the factors and situations that may influence and coordinate employee action allows the management accountant to adapt the services to offer to the realities of human behavior. The literature on motivation identifies five theories of motivation: the need theory, the two-factor theory, the value/expectancy theory, the achievement theory, and the inequity theory. Each of these theories identifies what factors within the individual and his or her environment activate high performance, or attempts to explain and describe the process of how behavior is activated, what directs it, and how it is controlled and stopped. Let us examine each of these theories of motivation and their implications for management accounting.

Need Theory

Originally advanced by Abraham Maslow, need theory holds that people are motivated to satisfy a "hierarchy" of needs.[21] These needs are as follows (in ascending order of prepotency):

Exhibit 3.1

Proposed Objectives and Concepts for Social Accounting

Objective 1

An objective of corporate social accounting is to identify and measure the periodic net social contribution of an individual firm, which includes not only the costs and benefits internalized to the firm, but also those arising from externalities affecting different social segments.

Objective 2

An objective of corporate social accounting is to help determine whether an individual firm's strategies and practices which directly affect the relative resource and power status of individuals, communities, social segments and generations are consistent with widely shared social priorities, on the one hand, and individuals' legitimate aspirations, on the other.

Objective 3

An objective of corporate social accounting is to make available in an optimal manner, to all social constituents, relevant information on a firm's goals, policies, programs, performance and contributions to social goals. Relevant information is that which provides for public accountability and also facilitates public decision making regarding social choices and social resource allocation. Optimality implies a cost/benefit-effective reporting strategy which also optimally balances potential information conflicts among the various social constituents of a firm.

Concept 1

A *social transaction* represents a firm's utilization or delivery of a socioenvironmental resource which affects the absolute or relative interests of the firm's various social constituents and which is not processed through the market place.

Concept 2

Social overheads (returns) represent the sacrifice (benefit) to society from those resources consumed (added) by a firm as a result of its social transactions. In other words, social overheads is the measured value of a firm's negative externalities, and social returns is the measured value of its positive externalities.

Concept 3

Social income represents the periodic net social contribution of a firm. It is computed as the algebraic sum of the firm's traditionally measured net income, its aggregate social overheads and its aggregate social returns.

Concept 4

Social constituents are the different distinct social groups (implied in the second objective and expressed in the third objective of social accounting) with whom a firm is presumed to have a social contract.

Concept 5

Social equity is a measure of the aggregate changes in the claims which each social constituent is presumed to have in the firm.

Concept 6

> *Net social asset* of a firm is a measure of its aggregate nonmarket contribution to the society's well being less its nonmarket depletion of the society's resources during the life of the firm.

Source: Kavasseri V. Ramanathan, "Towards a Theory of Corporate Social Accounting," *The Accounting Review* (July 1976): 527. Reprinted with permission.

1. The physiological needs: food, shelter, warmth, and other bodily wants.
2. The safety needs: security and protection.
3. The need for love and belongingness: desire to both give and receive love and friendship.
4. The need for esteem: self-respect and the respect of others.
5. The self-actualization need:" What a man can be, he must be."

Thus, individuals strive to satisfy these needs in a sequential fashion, starting with the physiological needs. The process of deprivation-domination-gratification-activation continues until the self-actualization need has been activated. This suggests that once the basic physiological and safety needs are satisfied, individuals will respond better to rewards leading to self-respect and self-respect and self-actualization than to economic rewards, which are primarily related to the satisfaction of lower-level needs. What this implies for information management is that assuming individuals in the organization are well paid, the emphasis should be on the introduction of information management techniques, in general, and control techniques, in particular, that are consistent with the satisfaction of higher-level needs. This view is also shared by E. H. Caplan when he states that "it may be more important to concentrate on the development of organizational structures, leadership practices, and control systems which are consistent with satisfaction of the higher level needs."[22]

Two-Factor Theory

In a series of studies, F. Herzberg and his associates developed the "motivation hygiene" theory.[23] Briefly, they found two factors affecting a job situation, which they labeled *satisfiers* and *dissatisfiers.* The satisfiers were related to the nature of the work itself and to rewords that flowed directly from the performance of that work: (1) perceived opportunity for achievement on the job, (2) recognition, (3) a sense of performing interesting and important work, (4) responsibility, and (5) advancement. The dissatisfiers were related to the context rather than the content of the job: (1) company policies that foster ineffectiveness, (2) incompetent supervision, (3) interpersonal relations, (4) working conditions, (5) salaries, (6) status, and (7) job security. The satisfiers were classified as "motivators" and dissatisfiers as "hygiene" factors.

According to Herzberg, the satisfiers contribute very little to job dissatisfaction; and conversely, the dissatisfiers contribute very little to job satisfaction. Similarly, motivation to work is created by the satisfaction of the individual's needs for the satisfiers and not from an elimination of the dissatisfiers. The implications of Herzberg's theory for management accounting techniques should focus on better measurement and reporting of achievement, recognition, work, responsibility, and advancement. Second, given that the key to motivation is to make jobs more meaningful, management accounting techniques should focus on job enrichment. Job enrichment is the attempt by managers to design task in such a way as to affect employees' positive feelings about their job and to build in the opportunity for personal achievement, recognition, challenge, and personal growth. It gives the employees a greater amount of responsibility in carrying out complete tasks and insures a timely feedback on their performance.[24] Martin Evans suggests several steps to insure job enrichment of relevance to management accounting:[25]

1. Eliminating controls from the job while keeping accountability.
2. Increasing the individual's accountability for his or her job.
3. Providing each individual with a complete and natural work module (or elements of work).
4. Allowing greater job freedom for an individual's own work.
5. Providing timely feedbacks on performance to the employee instead of the supervisor.
6. Improving old tasks and introducing new tasks.
7. Assigning specific tasks so the employee can develop expertise in performing them.

Value/Expectancy Theory

The theories of Maslow, McClelland, and Herzberg are content theories in the sense that they attempt to identify what factors within the individual and the individual's environment induce high performance. The value/expectancy theory is a process theory in the sense that it attempts to explain and describe the process of how behavior is initiated, maintained, and terminated.

Originally developed by K. Lewin,[26] and later specially applied to motivation to work by V. H. Vroom,[27] the basic tenet of the value/expectancy theory is that an individual chooses personal behavior on the basis of: (1) expectations that such behavior will result in a specific outcome, and (2) the sum of the valences—that is, personal utilities or rewards, derived from the outcome. Vroom advances the following theoretical proposition:

> The force on a person (motive) to perform a given act is based on the weighted value (or utility) of all the possible outcomes of the act multiplied by the perceived usefulness of the given act in the attainment of these outcomes. Whenever an individual chooses between alternatives that involve certain outcomes, it seems clear that his behavior is affected not only by his preferences among outcomes, but also by the degree to which he believes these outcomes to be probable.[28]

Hence, an individual's motivation may be expressed as:

$$M = \sum[(E \rightarrow O)(V)]$$

where

E = Effort

O = Outcome

V = Value placed on the outcome

The above expression may be reformulated to include both an effort-performance linkage and a performance-reward linkage. The new model will include two expectancies. The first one refers to the probability that the effort will lead to a task accomplishment or performance. The second one refers the probability that the task accomplishment will result in the desired outcomes. Hence, the individual's motivation may also be expressed as:

$$M = [(E \rightarrow P) \sum[(P \rightarrow O)(V)]$$

where

P = Performance

L. W. Porter and E. E. Lawler have extended the value/ expectancy theory by arguing that poor performance may result if abilities are lacking and the individual's role perceptions are erroneous.[29] Thus, for preferences and expectations to affect performance, adequate ability and accurate role perceptions are necessary.

R. J. House's formulation of the model can be expressed as follows:[30]

$$M = V_b + P_i (V_a + \sum_{i=1}^{n} P_2 EV_i)$$

where

i	=	1, 2, ..., n
M	=	Motivation to work

IV_a = Intrinsic valence associated with successful performance of the task

IV_b = Intrinsic valence associated with goal-directed behavior

EV_i = Extrinsic valences associated with the ith extrinsic reward contingent on work-goal accomplishment

P_i = The expectancy that goal-directed behavior will accomplish the work goal (a given level of specified performance); the measure's range is (-1, +1)

P_{2i} = The expectancy that work-goal accomplishment will lead to the ith extrinsic reward; the measure's range is (-1, +1)

This formulation shows some of the implications of expectancy theory for information management. Appropriate information management techniques may be chosen to affect the independent variables of the model in the following ways:

1. By determining what extrinsic rewards (EV_i) follow work-goal accomplishment.
2. By increasing through timely reports the individual's expectancy (P_{2i}) that work-goal accomplishment leads to extrinsic rewards.

3. By increasing the intrinsic valence associated with work-goal accomplishment (IV_a) through a greater role of the individual in goal-setting and task-directed effort.

4. By recognizing and supporting the individual's effort thereby influencing P_i.

5. By increasing the net intrinsic valences associated with goal-directed behavior (IV_b)

Achievement Theory

The concept of "achievement motive" was first introduced by McClelland, Atkinson, and their associateds.[31] It is based on the desire of people to be challenged and to be innovative and adopt an "achievement-oriented behavior" — that is, a behavior directed toward meeting a standard of excellence. McClelland viewed the motive to achieve as distinct from acquisitiveness for money, except insofar as money is considered a symbol of achievement. Using the Thematic Apperception Test (TAT) to measure three distinct needs (need for achievement, need for power, and need for affiliation), he found the achievement level to be correlated with personality and cultural variables.

The achievement-oriented individual likes to assume responsibility for individual achievement, seeks challenging tasks, and takes calculated risks depending on the probabilities of success. Therefore,

> He will take small risks for tasks serving as stepping stones for future rewards, take intermediate risks for

> tasks offering opportunities for achievement, and will attempt to find situations falling somewhere between the two extremes, providing the highest probability of success, and hence maximizing his sense of personal achievement.

According to the theory, the individuals will particularly behave in an achievement-oriented way in situations that enable them to strive for a standard of excellence, require the use of skills, present a challenge, and allow the individuals to appraise their performance. Accordingly, Atkinson stated that the strength of one's tendency to succeed at a task (T_s)

> is a multiplicative function of three variables: motive to achieve success (M_s) which is conceived as a relatively general and stable disposition of personality and measured in terms of need for achievement; and two other variables which represent the effect of the intermediate environment–the strength of expectancy (or subjective probability) that performance of a task will be followed by success (P_s) and the relative attractiveness of success of that particular activity, which is called the incentive of success (I_s). I_s assumed to be greater the more difficult the task.[32]

Another important contention of the theory is that all motives are learned, including the achievement motive. As a result, the high achiever is experienced in making maximizing decisions, is less affected by anxiety, and proceeds in an efficient way in any endeavor.

What these contentions imply for information management is: (1) the necessity of constructing ways of developing the achievement motive at all managerial levels, and (2) the need to introduce information management techniques and to report management information that encourages and facilitates the performance of high achievers.

Inequity Theory

Elaine Walster, Stacey Adams, and their colleagues have advanced that individuals in a relationship have two motives: to maximize their own gains and to maintain equity in the relationship.[33] Inequity results when a person's rewards from a relationship are not proportional to what that person has put in the relationship. More explicitly, inequity theory is based on the premise that when individuals compare their own situations with other situations and have a feeling of inequity, in terms of feeling either under rewarded or over rewarded for their contributions, they experience increased tension an strive to reduce it. Hence, overpaid workers will increase their efforts by producing more as a way of reducing inequity, while underpaid workers will produce less to achieve a contribution-reward balance. Other methods of restoring equity may be used also. Walster et al. state that individuals can restore actual equity by altering either their own payoffs or those of other participants. Similarly, a psychological equity can be restored when individuals change their perceptions of either rewards or contributions so that their contributions appear greater or lower than originally thought. They may also restore equity by quitting their jobs, severing relationships with comparison persons, or by forcing comparison persons to leave the field.

The inequity theory suggests, then, that rewards must appear to the employees to be fair or equitable. An appeal to equity norms can be used to reduce conflict. The role of information management in restoring equity is in insuring correct and accurate measurement and reporting of performance and the corresponding rewards. To avoid creating feelings of inequity, the methods of measuring performance and rewards should be made public to the employees.

MODELS OF DECISION MAKING

Information management necessitates a good grasp of decision making in organizations. The identification of the decision-making models most relevant to particular contexts and most preferred by particular individuals allows the management accountant to adapt the services to offer to the realities of the decision situation. The literature on decision making identifies five main perspectives: the "rational" manager view, the "satisficing" process-oriented view, the organizational procedures view, the political view, and the individual differences perspective.[34]

Before analyzing each of these models, it is appropriate to mention the excellent analysis of the Cuban missile crisis by G. T. Allison using three of these models: the rational actor view, the organizational procedures view, and the political view.[35] Addressing the central issues of the crisis from one of the three perspectives "lead[s] one to see, emphasize, and worry about quite different aspects of events."[36] By analogy, addressing management issues from any of the five perspectives leads one to have different perceptions and understanding of events and place on the management accountant different demands for services. Let us examine each of these models and its importance to management accounting.

The Rational View

The rational view of decision making is a normative model that refers to a consistent value-maximizing choice process in the presence of specific constraints. This process may be summarized as follows:

1. Individuals assume that there is a set of alternative acts or courses of action displayed before them in a particular situation.
2. They associate a set of possible outcomes or consequences with the set of possible acts.
3. They have a preference ordering over the consequences or payoff function that allows them to rank the consequences and select that act which ranks highest in their payoff function.

This view is used and relied upon as the model of the "economic man" in neoclassical economic theory and as the model of the "rational man" in game theory and statistical decision theory. Both make optimal choices in the presence of well-defined specific constraints.

As a defense of the rational view of decision making, one of the two assumptions has been made. On the one hand, there is the assumption of comprehensive rationality where individuals have perfect knowledge of all alternative acts, all the consequences, and the corresponding payoff function. On the other hand, there is the assumption of limited rationality with its inherent restricted claim on "optimal choice." Whatever the assumptions, the rational view of decision making requires the management accountant to define all the possibilities in terms of acts, consequences, and payoff function, and to evaluate the costs and benefits associated with rational decision making.

The rational view of decision making, although normative and rigorous, has been criticized as being descriptively unrealistic. H. A. Simon, in particular, advanced the principle of bounded rationality of the human decision maker:

> When the limits to rationality are viewed from the individual's standpoint, they fall into three categories: he is limited by his values and conceptions of purpose, which may diverge from the organizational goals; he is limited by the extent of his knowledge and information. The individual can be rational in terms of the organization's goals only to the extent that he is able to pursue a particular course of action, he has a correct conception of the goal of the action, and he is correctly informed

> about the conditions surrounding his action. Within the boundaries laid down by these factors, his choices are rational-goal oriented.[37]

In replacement of the "economic man," Simon suggests the notion of the "administrative" or "satisficing" man as more representative of what is in decision making.

The Satisficing and Process-Oriented View

The satisficing and process-oriented view of decision making is a descriptive model that maintains that the administrative individual satisfices rather than optimizes when making most decisions. Thus, rather than searching the haystack for the sharpest needle, the objective of the administrative man is to find one sharp enough to sew with.[38] Simon summarizes the assumptions of the satisficer's theory as follows:

> In actual organizational practice, no one attempts to find an optimal solution for the whole problem. Instead, various particular decisions, or groups of decisions, within the whole complex are made by specialized members or units of the organization. In making these particular decisions, the specialized units do not solve the whole problem but find a "satisfactory" solution for one or more subproblems, where some of the effects of the solution on other parts of the system are incorporated in the definition of "satisfactory."[39]

Thus, the satisficing man makes a decision-making choice in the context of a simplified view of the real situation. Simon introduces a concept of "subjective rationality" as a challenge to the concept of "objective rationality" advocated by the rational view of decision making. Subjective rationality depends on the individual's personal values. Thus, an objectively rational decision calls for a maximizing behavior given values in a specific situation, while a subjectively rational decision calls for maximizing attainment relative to the actual knowledge of the individual.[40] To be able to satisfice, the individual's strategies will consist essentially of heuristics or rules of thumb that meet a subjective minimum standard with respect to the things being sought.

That managers satisfice rather than optimize, refer to subjective rather than objective rationality, and rely on their heuristics places distinctive demands on the management accountant. To be able to service managers and facilitate their decision-making process, an understanding of their heuristics is essential. It is not an insurmountable task, given the general evidence suggesting how simple and how few are the heuristics used by managers. It also implies a good working relationship between managers and management accountants.

The Organizational Procedures View

The organizational procedures view of decision making is a descriptive model that maintains that individuals comply with an act according to a fixed set of standard operating procedures and programs. They make their choice in terms of goals and on the basis of expectations. R. M. Cyert and J. G. March perceive the organization as a coalition of individuals with different demands, priorities, goals, focus of attention, and competencies.[41] Decision making within the organization requires bargaining among the coalition members, resulting in de facto agreements and standard procedures for dealing with problematic situations.

Thus, individuals will act according to standard patterns of behavior established in their particular organizational unit to achieve its stated goals. What results in the organization is: (1) a permanent goal conflict between the units with possibly the dominant coalition imposing its independent constraints, (2) a quasi resolution of conflict marked by a sequential attention to problems, (3) uncertainty avoidance, (4) problematic search where the search is triggered by a specific problem and motivated to finding a solution to the problem, and (5) organizational learning leading to changes in goals, expectations, and standard procedures.

This process-oriented view of decision making has been applied with some success to simulate the working of a retail department store by Cyert and March,[42] the trust investment process used by officers in a bank by G. E. Clarkson,[43] the behavior of government units in municipal budgeting by John Crecine,[44] and the foreign investment decision process of business by Lair Aharoni.[45]

That managers may belong to coalitions that reply on programs and standard procedures places distinctive demands on management accountants. These coalitions and their standard procedures should be identified by management accountants to be able to service managers and facilitate their decision making. This implies that management accountants must be careful not to be identified with any of these coalitions, but as support agents providing the necessary information for an efficient resolution of problems. Following P. R. Lawrence and J. W. Lorsch's[46] appeal for a balance between integration and differentiation within complex organizations, management accountants may act as integrating agents between the subunits of the organization.

The Political View

The political view of decision making is a descriptive model that maintains that decisions are due partly to political processes. In this process, different groups committed to different courses of action interact and arrive at decisions through the "pulling and hauling that is politics."[47] The differences between this view and the rational and process views are summarized by Allison as follows: "what moves the chess pieces is not simply the reasons that support a course of action or the routines of organizations that enact an alternative but the power and skill of proponents and opponents of the action in itself."[48] Thus, each individual in the firm is a player in a competitive game called politics, where persuasion, accommodation, bargaining, and the constant search for support are the determinants of decision making. This may be justified because

> Managers [government leaders] have competitive, not homogeneous interests; priorities and perceptions are shaped by positions; problems are much more varied than straight-forward strategic issues; management of piecemeal streams of decisions is more important than steady-state choices; making sure that management

> [the government] does what is decided is more difficult than selecting the preferred solution.[49] (Allison's original words are shown in brackets.)

This political view resulted in the concept of incremental change advanced mainly by C. W. Lindblom.[50] According to this view, labeled as "the art of the possible," managers attack rather than solve problems incrementally through "successive limited comparisons."

That mangers may be motivated by political positions and disagree with other political positions in the firm, that they may favor managing through incremental muddling rather than comprehensive, satisfactory, or procedural choice is very relevant for the management accountant and should not be ignored. The acceptance and use of either information management techniques or information suggested by the management accountant is very much a function of the political dimensions existing in the firm.

The Individual Differences View

The individual differences view maintains that individuals have specific decision-making styles appropriate for some cases and less so for others. This view emerged from the recognition in psychology of the concept of cognitive style as a hypothetical construct to explain the mediation process between stimuli and responses. Five approaches have been reported for the study of cognitive style: authoritarianism, dogmatism, cognitive complexity, integrative complexity, and field dependence.[51]

1. Authoritarianism arose from the focus by T. W. Adorno et al. on the relationship between personality, antidemocratic attitudes, and behavior.[52] They were primarily interested in individuals whose way of thinking made them susceptible to antidemocratic propaganda. Two of the behavioral correlates of authoritarianism—regidity and intolerance of ambiguity—were reflections of an underlying cognitive style. For example, J. Dermer investigated the relationship between intolerance of ambiguity and subjective cue usage.[53] His result showed a significant positive correlation between intolerance of ambiguity and the amount of information perceived to be important.

2. Dogmatism arose from M. Rokeach's efforts to develop a structurally based measure of authoritarianism to replace the content-based measure developed by Adorno and his colleagues.[54] His interest was in developing a measure of cognitive style that would be independent of the content of thought.

3. Cognitive complexity as introduced by G. A. Kelly[55] and J. Bieri et al.[56] focuses on the psychological dimensions that individuals use to structure their environments and to differentiate the behavior of others. The more cognitively complex individuals are assumed to have a greater number of dimensions available with which to construe the behavior of others than the less cognitively complex persons. Another clarification of decision makers in the literature is made in terms of two cognitive styles: heuristic and analytic. Based on terms and meanings used by Jan Huysmans,[57] they may be defined as follows: Analytic decision makers reduce problem situations to a more or less explicit, often quantitative, model as a basis for their decision. Heuristic decision makers refer instead to common sense, intuition, and

unquantified feelings about future development as they apply to the totality of the situation as an organic whole rather than a built from clearly identifiable parts. Huysman's findings show particularly that cognitive style may operate as an effective constraint on the implementation of operations research recommendations, and that operations researchers perceive their own analytic style as self-evident and tend to ignore the impact of cognitive style on the acceptance and use of analytic techniques. Similarly, in an experimental study of the relationship between different information structures, decision approaches, and learning patterns, T. Mock, T. Estrin, and M. Vasarhelyi[58] found that analytics significantly outperformed heuristics in terms of profit and decision time.

4. Integrative complexity as presented by O. J. Harvey et al.,[59] and later expanded by H. M. Schroder et al.,[60] results from the view that people engage in two activities in processing sensory input: differentiation and integration. Differentiation refers to the individual's ability to place stimuli along dimensions. Integration refers to the individual's ability to employ complex rules to combine these dimensions. Then a person low on both activities is said to be concrete, while a person high on both activities is said to be abstract. The continuum from concrete to abstract is referred to as an integrative or conceptual complexity. To the concept of integrative complexity is usually added the concept of environmental complexity and the level of information processing. It is expressed by the "U-Curve Hypothesis" as depicted in Exhibit 3..2. As the level of information processing increases and reaches a maximum level at an optimal level of environmental complexity beyond which it begins to decrease.[61] H. M. Schroder et al. extended the concept of the inverted U-shaped curve to

the study of integrative complexity. The differences between the concrete and the abstract individual are also shown in Exhibit 4.2. The more abstract the individual, the higher the maximum level of information processing.

5. Finally, field dependence as presented by H. A. Witkin and his associates is a measure of the extent of differentiation in the area of perception.[62] Field-dependent individuals tend to perceive the overall organization of a field and are relatively unable to perceive parts of the field as discrete. Field-independent individuals, however, tend to perceive parts of the filed as discrete from organized parts rather than fused with it.

Exhibit 3.2

Functioning of Concrete and Abstract Individuals in Relation to Environmental Complexity

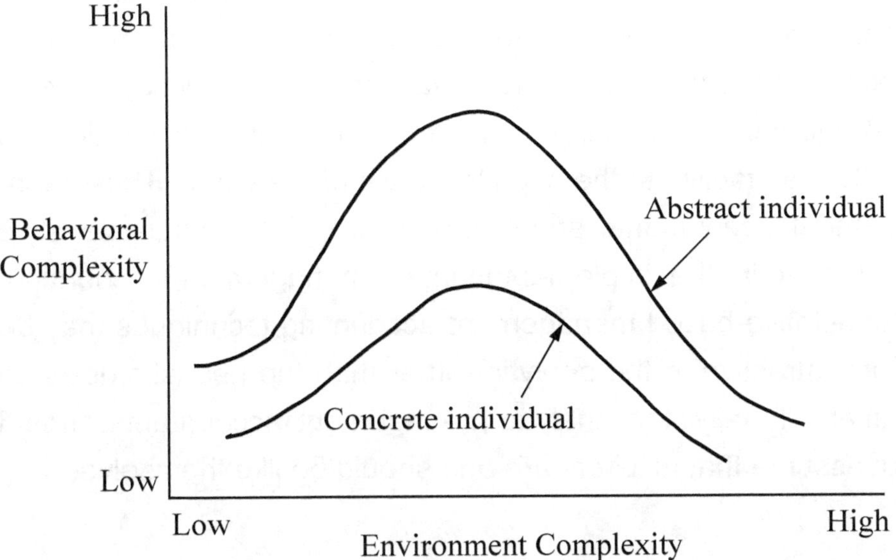

That managers have specific cognitive styles in terms of authoritarianism, dogmatism, cognitive complexity, integrative complexity, and filed dependence, which give them specific styles of decision making, has strong implications for management accounting. First, management accounting reports should be compatible with the cognitive structures of its users. They should be designed on the basis of realistic assumptions about the users' decision styles. Second, the utilization and the acceptance of management accounting techniques and information depend on their suitability to the cognitive style of the users. Thus, management accountants should be aware of the cognitive style constraint in the implementation of management accounting. Quantitative-based management accounting techniques may be more attractive to the analytic rather than the heuristic decision makers. Finally, the analytic management accountants should not assume that all users are and should be like themselves.

HEURISTICS AND BIASES

Research in behavioral decision theory suggests that individuals seem to employ heuristics and biases in order to reduce complete cognitive processes to simpler judgmental obligations that are more manageable. Research in behavioral information has tried to verify the existence of these heuristics and biases in judgments in an information ng setting. To date, this type of research has examined the following heuristics: representativeness, availability, confirmation bias, anchoring and adjustment, the conjunction fallacy, hindsight bias, illusory correlation, and the Weber-Fechner law. That managers resort to these heuristics in making professional and business judgments also has strong implications for management accounting. Management accountants have to take these heuristics into account when devising the content and format of management accounting reports. To understand the differences in information needs, the various types of heuristics are explicated.

Representativeness

A frequent heuristic in probability assessment appears to be representativeness. "A person who follows this heuristic evaluates the probability of an uncertain event, or a sample, by the degree to which it is: (i) similar in essential properties to its parent population; and (ii) reflects the salient features of the process by which it is generated."[63] According to this heuristic, a person will estimate the probability that subject A belongs to class B by the extent to which A resembles B. This heuristic, where class membership is assessed by the degree of its similarity to a stereotypical class member, has been found to lead to the following systematic biases in probability estimation:[64]

- Insensitivity to prior probability or base rate
- Insensitivity to the impact of sample size on the variance of the sampling distribution
- Misperception of the likelihood of different sequences resulting from a random process
- Insensitivity to the predictability of data

The neglect of the base rate was investigated a number of times, varying base rates, problem content, information order, and response mode.[65] The results confirmed the findings that base rates were ignored. When other experiments were used within subject experimental designs rather than between subjects, the finds showed that base rates were not ignored, in the sense that the subjects modified their judgments in the appropriate direction as the base rate was changed.[66]

Where the base rate was neglected, it was attributed to the fact that people lacked good schemata for working with probabilistic information,[67] and the "abstract, pallid, and remote" nature of the base rate contrasted to the generally "concrete, vivid, and salient" character of individuating information.[68]

In fact, three situations characterize the base rate fallacy case[69]:

1. People tend to reply on the base rate in making their judgments when case-specific evidence doesn't suggest a hypothesis (i.e., is not diagnostic and therefore not informative).[70]

2. People ignore the base rate when case-specific evidence strongly favors a particular hypothesis (i.e., is not diagnostic and therefore not informative).[71]

3. People rely on the base rates when the experimental case wording or format make them appear causal[72] or specific.[73] This naturally follows from the findings that different framings of short cases will provide different

results[74] and the suggestion by Tversky and Kahneman[75] that in the preliminary analysis of a decision problem, the decision maker frames the effective acts, contingencies, and outcomes: "Framing is controlled by the manner in which the choice problem is presented as well as by norms, habits and expectancies of the decision maker."[76]

Availability

Availability of information is argued to be an important clue that people use in making judgments. It has been considered as a bias whereby people make a probabilistic judgment on an event by the ease with which similar events are recalled. "A person is said to employ the availability heuristic whenever he estimates frequency or probability of the case with which instances or complications can be brought to mind."[77] That is, frequent events are easier to recall than infrequent ones, making availability a valid cue for the assessment of frequency and probability. Availability is also influenced by factors unrelated to likelihood, such as familiarity, recency, and emotional saliency and imaginability. S. Lichtenstein et al. asked their subjects to compare the frequency of occurrence of pairs of lethal events and found that they overestimated the relative frequency of diseases or causes of death that are much publicized.[78] What seems apparent is that emphasis on some aspects in the environment affects judgment by making it easier to recall instances and estimate their frequency.

Michael Ross and Fiore Sicoly postulated that an egocentric bias in availability of information in memory could produce biased attribution of responsibility for a joint product because of significant processes that may be operating to increase the availability of one's own contributions: selective encoding and storage of information, differential retrieval, informational disparities, and motivational influences.[79] Three experiments confirmed the prevalence of self-centered biases in availability and judgments of responsibility.

> In everyday life these egocentric tendencies may be overlooked when joint endeavors do not require explicit allocations of responsibility. If allocations are stated distinctly, however, there is a potential for discussion, and individuals are unlikely to realize their differences in judgment could arise from honest evaluations that are differentially available.[80]

Confirmation Bias

It is an accepted normative view of scientific inference that disconfirmation and testing of alternative hypotheses have major roles. More particularly, Karl Popper's philosophy of science centers around the concept of disconfirmation or refutation.[81] He maintained that hypotheses can be disconfirmed only by evidence and never confirmed. J.R. Platt also argued that successive generations of alternative hypotheses should be disconfirmed—a strategy he labels "strong inference."[82]

Popper asserted that the purpose of science is not the verification but the falsification of theories.[83] The falsification can be achieved by deductive logic. If one adopts a rationalist view of humanity, then deductive logic is a necessary and natural part of human thought.[84] The behaviorist view would argue that the use of logical knowledge depends on whether or not the appropriate reinforcement contingencies have been applied.[85]

People are generally presented with conditional relationships between propositions that may be represented as "if *p*, then *q*," where *p* is the antecedent and *q* is the consequent. A typical deductive reasoning problem is to entertain alternative hypotheses with respect to the truth or the falsity of the rule. Given *p, q, p'* (not *p*) and *q*' (not *q*), the problem of deciding whether the rule "if *p,* then *q"* is true or false becomes a deductive reasoning problem. The selection may be accomplished using either a verification or falsification principle, depending on the degree of weight,[86] and as follows:

- A subject with no insight will select the options that verify the rule. That is, they will choose *p* or *p* and *q*.
- A subject with partial insight will appreciate the need to select potential falsifiers, but only choose options that could only verify. *p'* will be considered *irrelevant* because it should neither verify nor falsify. All other options will be chosen (i.e., *p, q,* and *q*') because they could either verify, falsify, or both.
- A subject with complete insight will select only the options that could falsify. That is, *p* and *q'* will be chosen.

Which strategies will be used has been the subject of experiments using either abstract or thematic problems, with the evidence showing only 10 percent of the subjects capable of solving the problem using the falsification principle.[87] The results were consistent with undergraduates as well as more sophisticated subjects (e.g., Ph.D. psychologists and statisticians)[88], and with abstract as well as thematic tasks.[89]

Which of these three strategies will be used by the accountant? The auditor's concern is mainly with verification—the examination of financial data for the purpose of judging the faithfulness with which they portray events and conditions. P.K. Mautz and H. A. Sharaf emphatically state the focus on verification:

> In the business world, the act of verification is the trade of auditors, both internal and external. This philosophical truth about the necessity of verification is so well accepted that the business world has adopted a general practice of submitting such propositions to a verification process before they are given any serious consideration for many purposes. This verification consideration takes many forms; sometimes it is the continuous examination of procedures and data performed by an internal audit staff, sometimes the annual examination of an independent auditor, sometimes the investigation of an Internal Revenue Agent. Whatever the form, the importance and fact of verification are well accepted.[90]

Therefore, while deductive logic dictates the use of falsification in a deductive reasoning task, the emphasis on verification in auditing will lead the auditors to rely on a verification principle.

A. Belkaoui examined the use of logical knowledge in deductive reasoning by students and auditors.[91] One abstract and two thematic tasks were used and subjects were asked to test the truth or falsity of an implication rule. The results in the abstract test verified the dominance of the verification principle rather than the falsification principle for both students and auditors. No thematic effect was observed as the use of thematic effects showed a worsening of the falsification principle. In addition, the strong results on the dominance of the verification principle were found to be independent of the level of education, affiliation with a given accounting firm, positing in the firm, years of experience as an auditor, years of application with the firm, or age of the subjects. While there is strong evidence both an accounting and psychology for this "confirmation bias," J. Klayman and Y.-W. Ha showed that many phenomena labeled confirmation bias are better understood in terms of a general "positive test strategy."[92] In addition, confirmation bias has meant different things to different researchers. Examples include the findings that people pay undue attention to the frequency of occurrence of two events, while underweighting instances in which one event occurs without the other;[93] the findings that people tend to discredit or reinterpret information counter to a hypothesis they hold;[94] and the findings that people may conduct "biased" tests that pose little risk of producing disconfirming results.[95]

Anchoring and Adjustment

In many situations, people make estimates by thinking of an internal value or "anchor" that is suggested by the formulation of the task or as a result of partial computation, and then make some adjustment to it to yield the final answer. This heuristic has been termed "anchoring and adjustment." For example, if a purchasing agent is asked to estimate next year's purchases, he may start with last year's purchases before making some adjustments to them to reflect new environmental conditions. Therefore, people starting from different anchors end up with different answers. In addition, this heuristic has been found to lead to the following systematic biases in probability estimation:[96]

- Insufficient adjustment
- Biases in the evaluation of conjunctive and disjunctive events—"the chain-like structure of conjunctions leads to overestimation, the funnel-like structure of disjunctions leads to underestimation"[97]
- Anchoring in the assessment of subjective probability distributions

P. Slovic also found evidence of anchoring in the subjective valuation of gambles.[98] Subjects finding a gamble basically attractive use the amount to win as an anchor, then adjust it downward to take into account the less-than-perfect chance of winning and the possibility of losing a small amount. The adjustment was insufficient and Slovic pointed out that it may be the reason why people price gambles inconsistently with straight choices between pairs of gambles where a monetary response is not required.

The anchoring heuristic was also observed in an experiment by M. Albert and H. Raiffa.[99] They asked subjects to give the

1st and 99th percentile values for various quantities of items. It amounted to asking the subjects to estimate the 98 percent confidence intervals for the population value of the various quantities. The evidence showed that, on average, the subject's 98 percent confidence intervals included the true value only 40-50 percent of the time.

The Conjunction Fallacy in Probability Judgment

The conjunction rule, a qualitative law of probability, specifies that the probability of a conjunction, *P(A & B)*, cannot exceed the probabilities of its constituents, *P(A)* and *P(B),* because the extension (or the possibility set) of the conjunction is included in the extension of its constituents. In other words,

$$P(A \& B) \leq \min[P(A), P(B)]$$

But intuitive judgments of probability are generally not extensional. People instead use a limited number of heuristics. The natural assessments of representativeness and availability do not conform to the extensional logic of probability theory. "In particular, a conjunction can be more representative than one of its constituents, and instances of a specific category can be easier to retrieve than instances of a more inclusive category."[100]

One would expect, therefore, that representativeness and availability will make a conjunction appear more probable than one of its constituents. Indeed, Tversky and Kahneman present convincing evidence that people often violate the conjunction rule of probability theory when assessing the joint probability of two evetns.[101] They showed that both sophisticated and naïve people, in many different substantive problems, often judge the conjunction of events to be larger than one of its components ("single violation") or as large as both of its components ("double violation"). Their experimental task included the following components:

A = the judged probability of an event *A* given model *M*

J = the judged probability of an event *B* given model *M*

A & *J* = the judged probability of the conjunction of *A* and *J* given model *M*

The violations to the conjunction rule were $B<J<A$ or $B<A<J$.

For example, they gave their subjects the following task: "Bill is 24 years old. He is intelligent, but unimaginative, compulsive, and generally lifeless. In school he was strong in mathematics. Please rank order the following statements by the degree to which Bill resembles the identical member of that class."

- Bill is a physician, who plays poker for a hobby.
- Bill is an architect.
- Bill is an accountant. (*A*)

- Bill plays jazz for a hobby. (*J*)
- Bill surfs for a hobby.
- Bill is a reporter.
- Bill is an accountant who plays jazz for a hobby. (*A* & *J*)
- Bill climbs mountains for a hobby.

The risk included (1) a model *M* (the description of Bill), (2) an event *A* similar to the description (Bill is an accountant), (3) a dissimilar event *J* (Bill plays jazz for a hobby), and (4) the conjunction of two events (event *A* and *J:* Bill is an accountant who plays jazz for a hobby). The subjects ranked the conjunctive event (*A* & *J*) as more probable than one of its constituents in this task as well as for other tasks in a variety of contexts using a number of different methods.

One explanation of this phenomenon may be derived from Tversky's feature-matching model, which suggests:[102]

$$S(a,b) = J(A\&B) - J(A - B) - J(B - A)$$

where

A&B = the feature that are common to both *A* and *B*

$A - B$	=	the feature that belong to *A* but not to *B*
$B - A$	=	the feature that belong to *B* but not to *A*
J	=	an interval scale measure of feature salience
S	=	an interval scale measure of similarity

The model stipulates that the addition of a common feature to the stimuli produces an increase in their judged similarity and probability while the addition of distinctive feature to either of the two produces a decrease in their judged similarity and probability. In the Tversky and Kahneman experiments the addition of event *A* with common features to the prototypical outcome of the description and event *J* with distinctive features led the subjects to rank conjunctive event (*A&J*) as more probable than *J* but not more than *A*. H. J. Einhorn provides a more formal representation of the conjunction fallacy.[103] More examinations of judgments of event conjunctions were provided in various studies.[104]

Hindsight Bias

The hindsight bias or hindsight illusions were studied by B. Fischhoff[105] and Fischhoff and R. Byeth.[106] Basically, hindsight bias stipulates that subjects who have a knowledge that an outcome has occurred give that outcome a higher prior probability of occurrence than subjects who do not have any knowledge of the outcome. Fischhoff explains as follows:

> In hindsight, people consistently exaggerate what could have been anticipated in foresight. They not only tend to view what has happened as inevitable, but also to view it as having appeared "relatively inevitable" before it happened. People believe that others should have been able to anticipate events much than was actually the case. They even misremember their own predictions so as to exaggerate in hindsight what they know in foresight.[107]

In addition, subjects seem to be unaware of the influence of outcome knowledge on assessed probabilities. As stated by Fischhoff: "Making sense out of what he is told about the past seems so natural and effortless a response that one may be unaware that outcome knowledge has had any effect at all on him."[108]

Hindsight bias was observed in experiments by Fischhoff[109] employing psychotherapy cases, by Slovic and Fischhoff[110] employing the outcomes of scientific experiments, and by Fischhoff and Byeth[111], Fischhoff[112], and G. Wood[113], employing general knowledge events. It was also observed in a number of medical settings involving judgments by nurses,[114] patients,[115] surgeons,[116] and physicians.[117]

Various arguments were provided to explain the hindsight bias. First, that outcome knowledge restructures memory.[118] R. Hogarth, for example, states:

> The knowledge that an event has occurred seems to restructure one's memory. Our memory of the past is not a memory of the uncertainties of the past, rather it is a reconstruction of past events in terms of what actually occurred. Furthermore, that past is structured in a way that makes some kind of coherent sense to the individual, for example, concerning the relationship between what actually happened and particular (but not all) antecedent events.[119]

Second, it stems from the difference between foresight and hindsight, with the first requiring more powers of imagination.

> Prediction requires considerable powers of imagination and both the ability and willingness to entertain several hypotheses simultaneously. Keeping one's options open is not a tidy exercise and can induce considerable anxiety.
>
> Postdiction or hindsight, on the other hand, requires little imagination and is an invitation to impose a causal structure on a sequence of past events. Furthermore, subjectively there is less uncertainty than in prediction problems concerning the events that "caused" what happened. One can believe any claim that seems plausible since it was seen to precede the event.[120]

Third, hindsight bias results from the limited availability of causal scenarios for alternative outcomes vis-à-vis scenarios for the reported outcome.[121]

Fourth, hindsight bias is a result of the individual's "fluency of diagnostic thinking."[122] In other words, outcome information makes possible the generation of a coherent story and what follows in terms of forward inference (i.e., prediction of outcomes) involves less uncertainty, given the reduction in the multiplicity of causation.

Fifth, hindsight bias is a result of motivating factors given that subjects, eager to preserve their self-images and how they are perceived by others, may be motivated to act as if they always knew what was going to occur.[123]

The hindsight bias raises a number of important issues with regard to judgments of the apparent failures (and successes) of others, distortions in memory, overcoming bias, and learning from experience.[124]

- With regard to judging others, hindsight makes it easier to judge the mistakes of others without considering that at the time a decision was made, it might have been quite reasonable.
- Distortions in memory result from hindsight bias. We may fail to blame people who make the wrong decision but get away with it.
- Fischhoff was able to "debias" distortions in memory caused by the knowledge of outcomes by giving the

subject knowledge of the true outcomes following the false information provided earlier. That created a stimulus capable of overcoming hindsight bias.

- The hindsight bias raise questions concerning the ability of people to learn from experience and to make predictions. [125]

Illusory Correlation and Contingency Judgments

Illusory correlation refers to the belief that two variables covary when, in fact, they do not. L. J. Chapman defined it as "the report by observers of a correlation between two classes of events which, in reality, (a) are not correlated, (b) are correlated to a lesser extent than reported, or (c) are correlated in the opposite direction from that which is reported." [126] In fact, Chapman and Chapman provided subjects with information concerning hypothetical mental patients, which included a clinical diagnosis and a drawing of a person made by the patient. [127] The drawings and symptom statements were combined in such a way that "each drawing occurred as often with on statement as another." [128] Therefore, no relationship existed between drawings and symptom statements. The subjects were then asked to estimate the frequency with which each diagnosis (e.g., suspiciousness or paranoia) had been accompanied by various features of the drawings (e.g., peculiar eyes). The results showed that the subjects markedly overestimated the frequency of co-occurrence of pairs commonly believed to exist by society, such as suspiciousness and peculiar eyes. Similar results in illusory correlations were provided by

Chapman and Chapman, [129] Golding and Rorer, [130] and Starr and Katkin. [131]

Illusory correlation studies point to the tendencies of finding nonexistent relationships.[132] studies of contingency judgments, however, point to sensitivity to certain relationships and not to others. If X_1 and X_2 represent two events like the presence or absence of cloud seeding, and Y_1 and Y_2 represent two other events like the presence absence of rain, then a contingency exists between *X* (cloud seeding) and *Y* (rain) to the extent that the probability of Y_1 given X_1 differs from the probability of Y_2 given X_2. A contingency exists between *X* and *Y* to the extent that *a/a+b* differs from *c/c+d. In contingency studies, subjects are generally asked to make a judgment J* about the degree to which the variables *X* and *Y* covary. The normative or objective covariation, *N,* is measured by organizing the data in a 2 X 2 joint frequency rule as in Exhibit 3.3 and applying one of the following correct data-integration rules:

N_1 (difference in diagnosis) = [a+d] – [b+c]

N_2 (delta coefficeint) = [a/(a+b)] – [c/(c+d)]

N_3 (contingency coeeficient) = $[X^2/(n+X^2)]^{1/2}$

N_4 (lambda coeffienct) = [max (*a,c*) + max (*b,d*)- max (*a+b,c+d*)]/[*n* – max(*a+b,c+d*)]

N_5 (phi coefficeint) = [*ad* – *bc*]/[(*a+c*)(*b+d*)(*a+b*)(*c+d*)]$^{1/2}$

Exhibit 3.3

2 × 2 Joint Frequency Table

	Presence of *Y*	Absence of *Y*
Presence of *X*	a	B
Absence of *X*	c	D

The correlation between *J*, the judgment about the degree to which the variables *X* and *Y* covary, and the data integration rule *N* is a measure of accuracy. The results of experiments point to the following:

- Subjects fail to appreciate that all four frequencies in the table in Exhibit 4.3 are required.[133]
- Subjects make errors in estimating cell frequencies when factors unrelated to frequency influence the availability of data retrieved from memory or produced by imagination.[134]
- Subjects concentrate on the number of positive confirmatory data of a cell *a* and occasionally cell *d*, and ignore or underestimate the number of disconfirmatory data.[134]
- Studies of manipulatory task difficulty indicate that the covariation judgment accuracy decreases as establishing a data set becomes more difficult.[136]

Weber-Fechner Law

The Weber-Fechner law suggests that a just noticeable difference is uniquely related to the standard for which it was established. More explicitly, given a standard *S* and a just noticeable difference *S*, then

Change in $S/S = K$ for all S

where

K = constant

In other words, the change in intensity of a stimulus that is necessary before it can be detected is a constant function of the amount of stimuli present. To measure the just noticeable difference, the method used is the method of constant stimulus differences. Under this method, subjects are presented with a standard, followed by a series of changes above and below the standard. The subjects are then asked to judge the pairs of stimuli. For the responses, three curves are drawn representing the relative frequency of judgments of larger, equal, and smaller for the different magnitudes of the comparison stimulus.

Accordingly, J Rose et al. made the hypothesis that people do respond to data stimuli as to sense stimuli and these stimuli obey the Weber-Fechner law. [137] They asked the subjects to judge whether a stock should sell for more than, less than, or the same as a series of comparison stocks, based on comparison of earnings-per-share (EPS) figures. The results showed that judgments of numerical stimuli could be represented by the Weber-Fechner law. In effect, the Weber ratios ranged from 6.6 to 7.0 percent of the standard stimulus across two experiments and two standards.

John Dickhaut and Ian Eggleton continued this line of research on the Weber-Fechner law of examining comparative judgments of numerical information, especially accounting information. [138]

Unlike the study by Rose et al., they manipulated the stated setting in which judgments were made, the sequence of data presentation, and the format in which standards and comparison stimuli were presented. The results showed that the subjects' perceptions of the data were consistent with the Weber-Fechner law. Examination of individual plots raised serious doubts about a similarity of the psychophysical process of comparing numerical stimuli. A second experiment was conducted followed by a questionnaire designed to elicit heuristics the subjects used in making similarity judgments. The results suggested that subjects used single decision rules, formulated either early in the task or possibly before the task was undertaken, applied inconsistently and defined as percentage functions of the expectations.

Magee and Dickhaut examined whether alternative compensation plans and the nature of the decision task condition the choice of heuristics. [139] Individuals' decision-making abilities in a cost-control setting were examined in an attempt to assess the effect of the compensation plan on these decisions. Based on an earlier study by Robert Magee, [140] they identified the heuristic to be used for each compensation plan. The results showed that alternative compensation plans condition the choice of heuristics. In addition, a questionnaire to elicit heuristics yielded results that were found to be related to differences in costs to the firm that would result from the different compensation plans. In short, alternation of the decision environment (specifically the compensation plan) influences the choice of heuristic and, ultimately, the costs incurred by an operating department. [141]

Other Heuristics

Various other heuristics have been extensively examined in psychology but not in accounting. There is a need for more accounting research to examine these untested heuristics in accounting. They include the following:

1. selective perception
2. frequency
3. concrete information
4. data presentation
5. inconsistency
6. conservatism
7. nonlinear extrapolation
8. law of small numbers
9. habit/"rules of thumb"
10. "best-guess" strategy
11. complexity in the decision environment
12. emotional stress in the decision environment
13. social pressures in the decision environment
14. consistency of information sources
15. question format

16. scale effects
17. wishful thinking
18. outcome-irrelevant learning structures
19. misperceptions of chance fluctuations (gambler's fallacy)
20. success/failure attributions
21. logical fallacies in recall

Exhibit 3.4

The Behavioral Foundations of Information Management

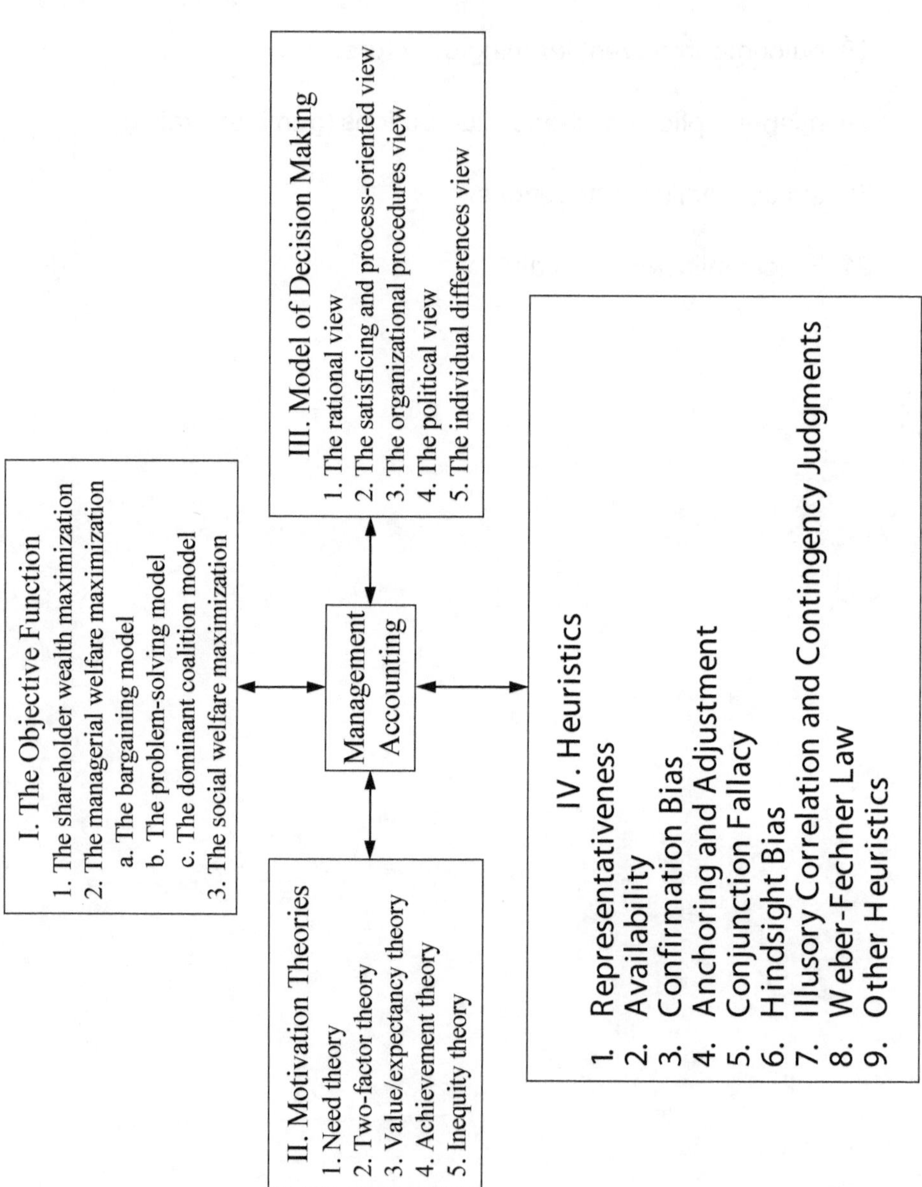

CONCLUSIONS

Information management rests on behavioral foundations. The type of objective function, motivation theories, heuristics, and the different models of decision making identify the factors likely to affect the behavior and performance of an individual within the organization (see Exhibit 2.4). First, management may either adopt the shareholder wealth maximization model, the managerial welfare model, or the social welfare model. The adoption of any model defines and restricts management to specific management techniques, attitudes, and behavior conductive to the accomplishment of the given objective. Second, the theories of motivation—namely, the need theory, the two-factor theory, the value/expectancy theory, the achievement theory, and the inequity theory—identify which environmental factors and management accounting techniques are susceptible to activate high performance or explain and describe the process of how desirable behavior may be initiated, encouraged, and even stopped. Third, the identification of the decision-making models employed by users in specific contexts may be of great help to the management accountant in adapting services to the users and the specific contexts. Five main perspectives of decision making were examined: the rational view, the satisficing process-oriented view, the organizational procedures view, the political view, and the individual differences view. Finally, the heuristics used by decision makers require different management reports in terms of informational content and format.

NOTES

1. Amitai Etzioni, *Modern Organizations* (Englewood Cliffs, N.J.: Prentice-Hall, 1964), p. 3.

2. Richard H. Hall, *Organizations: Structure and Process* (Englewold Cliffs, N.J.: Prentice-Hall, 1972), p.9.

3. V. Buck, "The Organization as a System of Constraints," in J. D. Thompson (ed.), *Approaches to Organization Design* (Pittsburgh: The University of Pittsburgh Press, 1966), p. 109.

4. J. D. Thompson, *Organizations in Action* (New York: McGraw-Hill, 1967), p. 18.

5. C. Perrow, "The Analysis of Goals in Complex Organizations," *American Sociological Review* 26 (1961): 854-866.

6. Etzioni, Modern Organizations, p. 7.

7. Chapman M. Findlay and G. A. Whitmore, "Beyond Shareholder Wealth Maximization," *Financial Management* (Winter 1974): 25-35.

8. E. Solomon, *The Theory of Financial Management* (New York: Columbia University Press, 1963), p. 24.

9. W. Baumol, *Business Behavior, Value and Growth* (New York: Macmillan, 1964).

10. R. Marris, The Economic Theory of Managerial Capitalism (London: Macmillan, 1964).

11. Papandreou, "Some Basic Issues in the Theory of the Firm," in B. Haley (ed.), *A Survey of Contemporary Economics,* (Homewood, Ill.: Richard D. Irwin, 1952). Also, O. Williamson, *The Economics of*

Discretionary Behavior: Managerial Objectives in the Theory of the Firm (Englewood Cliffs, N.J.: Prentice-Hall, 1964).

12. Branch, "Corporate Objectives and Market Performance," *Financial Management* (Summer 1973): 24-29.

13. Francine S. Hall. "Organizational Goals: The Status of Theory and Research," in J. Leslie Livingstone (ed.), *Managerial Accounting: The Behavioral Foundations* (Columbus, Ohio: Grid, 1975), pp. 1-29.

14. For an excellent presentation of these models, the reader is advised to examine the article by Hall in ibid.

15. Ibid., p. 17.

16. Ibid., p. 20.

17. Ibid., p. 23.

18. American Accounting Association, Committee on Measurement of Social Costs, "Report of the Committee on the Measurement of Social Costs," *The Accounting Review,* Supplement to Vol. 69 (1974): 100.

19. Ibid., pp. 101-102.

20. M. R. Jones (ed.), *Nebraska Symposium on Motivation* (Lincoln: University of Nebraska Press, 1955), p. 14.

21. Maslow, "A Dynamic Theory of Human Motivation," *Psychological Review* 50 (1943): 370-373.

22. E. H. Caplan, *Management Accounting and Behavioral Science* (Reading, Mass.: Addison-Wesley, 1971), p. 49.

23. F. Herzberg, B. Mausner, and B. Snyderman, *The Motivation to Work,* 2nd ed. (New York: John Wiley, 1959).

24. Jacques E. Powers, "Job Enrichment: How One Company Overcame the Obstacle," *Personnel* (May-June 1972): 8.

25. Martin G. Evans, "Herzberg's Two-Factor Theory of Motivation," *Personnel Journal* (January 1970): p. 33.

26. K. Lewin, *Field Theory and Social Science* (New York: Harper, 1951).

27. V. H. Vroom, *Work and Motivation* (New York: John Wiley, 1964).

28. Ibid., p. 18.

29. L. W. Porter and E. E. Lawler, *Managerial Attitudes and Performance* (Homewood, Ill.: Irwin-Dorsey, 1968).

30. R. J. House, "A Path-Goal Theory of Leader Effectiveness," *Administrative Science Quarterly* 16 (September 1971): 321-328.

31. D. C. McClelland, *Personally* (New York: William Sloan, 1951); *The Achieving Society* (New York: Van Nostrand, 1961). Also, J. W. Atkinson, "Toward Experimental Analysis of Human Motivation in Terms of Motives, Expectancies, and Incentives," in J. W. Atkinson (ed.), *Motives in Fantasy, Action and Society* (New York: Van Notstrand, 1958).

32. J. W. Atkinson, "Motivational Determinants of Risk Taking Behavior," *Psychological Review* 64 (1957): 14.

33. E. Walster, E. Berscheid, and G. W. Walster, "New Directions in Equity Research," *Journal of Personality and Social Psychology* 25 (1973): 151-176. Also, J. S. Adams, "Toward an Understanding of Inequity," *Journal of Abnormal and Social Psychology* 22 (1968): 1045-1053.

34. Peter G. Keen and Michael S. Scott Morton, *Decision Support Systems: An Organizational Perspective,* Addison-Wesley Series on Decision Support (Reading, Mass.: Addison-Wesley, 1978), pp. 62-63.

35. G. T. Allison, *Essence of a Decision* (Boston: Little, Brown, 1971).

36. Ibid., p. 5.

37. Herbert A. Simon, *Administrative Behavior,* 2nd ed. (New York: Macmillan, 1957), p. 241.

38. J. G. March and H. A. Simon, *Organizations* (New York: John Wiley, 1958), p. 141.

39. Simon, Administrative Behavior, p. 272.

40. Ibid., p. 76.

41. R. M. Cyert and J. G. March, *A Behavioral Theory of the Firm* (Englewood Cliffs, N.J.: Prentice-Hall, 1963).

42. Ibid.

43. G. E. Clarkson, "A Model of Trust Investment Behavior," in Cyert and March, *A Behavioral Theory of the Firm,* Ch. 10.

44. John P. Crecine, "Governmental Problem Solving," in *A Computer Simulation of Municipal Budgeting* (New York, 1969).

45. Lair Aharoni, The Foreign Investment Decision Process (Boston, 1966).

46. P. R. Lawrence and J. W. Lorsch, *Organization and Environment* (Cambridge, Mass.: Division of Research, Harvard Business School, 1967).

47. Allison, Essence of a Decision, p. 144.

48. Ibid., p. 145.

49. Ibid., p. 146.

50. C. W. Lindblom, "The Science of Muddling Through," *Public Administration Review* (Spring 1959): 79-88.

51. Kenneth R. Goldstein and Sheldon Blackman, *Cognitive Style: Five Approaches and Relevant Research* (New York: John Wiley, 1978), pp. 12-13.

52. T. W. Adomo, E. Frenkel-Brunswick, D. J. Levinson, and R. N. Sanford, *The Authoritarian Personality* (New York: Harper and Row, 1950).

53. J. Dermer, "Cognitive Characteristics and the Perceived Importance of Information," *The Accounting Review* (January 1973): 511-519.

54. M. Rokeach, *The Open and Closed Mind* (New York: Basic Books, 1960).

55. G. A. Kelly, *The Psychology of Personal Constructs,* 2 vols. (New York: W. W. Norton, 1955).

56. J. Bieri, "Cognitive Complexity and Personality Development," in O. J. Harvey (ed.), *Experience, Structure and Adaptability* (New York: Springer, 1966).

57. Jan H. B., Huysmans, "The Effectiveness of the Cognitive-Style Constraint in Implementing Operations Research proposals," *Management Science* (September 1970): 94-95.

58. T. Mock, T. Estrin, and M. Vasarhelyi, "Learning Patterns, Decision Approach and Value of Information," *Journal of Accounting Research* (Spring 1972): 129-153.

59. J. Harvey, D. E. Hunt, and H. M. Schroder, *Conceptual Systems and Personality Organizations* (New York: John Wiley, 1961).

60. H. M. Schroder, M. J. Driver, and S. Streufert, *Human Information Processing* (New York: Holt, Rinehart and Winston, 1967).

61. Ibid., p. 37.

62. H. A. Witkin, R. B. Dyks, H. F. Faterson, D. R. Goodenough, and S. A. Karyn, *Psychological Differentiation* (New York: John Wiley, 1962). Also, H. A. Witkin, H. B. Lewis, M. Hertzman, K. Machover, P. B. Meisner, and S. Wagner, *Personality Through Perception* (New York: Harper, 1954)

63. D. Kahneman and A. Tversky, "Subjective Probability: A Judgment of Representativeness," *Cognitive Psychology* (July 1972): 431.

64. Ibid., pp. 430-454; D. Kahneman and A. Tversky, "On the Psychology of Prediction," *Psychological Review* (July 1973): A. Tversky and D. Kahneman, "Judgment Under Uncertainty: Heuristics and Biases," *Science* (September 1974): 1124-1131.

65. M. Bar-Hiller, "The Base Rate Fallacy in Probability Judgments," *Acta Psychologica* (October 1980): pp. 211-233; D. Lyon and P. Slovic, "Dominance of Accuracy Information and Neglect of Base Rates in Probability Estimation," *Acta Psychologic* (January 1976): 287-298.

66. N. E. Airs and M. Maris, "Base-Rates Do Influence Social Judgments (But Not Optimally)" (working paper, University of Michigan,

1978): M. Mavis and I. Dovalina, "Base-Rates Can Affect Individual Predictions" (Working paper, University of Michigan, 1978).

67. R. E. Nisbett, R. Crandall, and H. Reed, "Popular Induction: Information is Not Necessarily Informative," In J. S. Carroll and J. W. Payne (eds.), *Cognitive and Social Behavior* (New York: Lawrence Erlbaum Associates, 1976).

68. R. E.Nisbett and E. Borgida, "Attribution and the Psychology of Prediction," *Journal of Personality and Social Psychology* (November 1975): 932-943.

69. D. Holt, "Evidence Integration in the Formation of Risk Assessments by Auditors and Bank Lending Officers" (unpublished dissertation, University of Michigan, January 1984).

70. B. Fischhoff and M. Bar-Hillel, "Diagnosticity and the Bae-Rate Effect," *Memory and Cognition* (July 1984): 402-410.

71. Ibid.

72. Tversky and D. Kahneman, "Evidential Impact on Base Rates,", in D. Kahneman, P. Slovic, and A. Tversky (eds.), *Judgment under Uncertainty: Heuristics and Biases* (New York: Cambridge university Press, 1982), pp. 153-160.

73. Bar-Hillel, "The Base Rate Fallacy in Probability Judgments."

74. P. Slovic, B. Fischhoff, and S. Lichtenstein, "Response Mode, Framing, and Information-Processing Effects in Risk Assessments," in R. Hogarth (ed.), *New Directions for Methodology of Social and Behavioral Science: Question Framing and Response Consistency*, no. 11, (San Francisco: Jossey-Bass, 1982), pp. 22-36.

75. Tversky and D. Kahneman, "Rational Choice and the Framing of Decisions," *Journal of Business* (October 1986).

76. Ibid., pp. 8251-8278.

77. Tversky and D. Kahneman, "Availability: A Heuristic for Judging Frequency and probability," *Cognitive Psychology* 5 (1973): 208.

78. S. Lichtenstein, P. Slovic, B. Fischhoff, M. Layman, and B. Combs, "Perceived Frequency of Lethal Events," *Decision Research Report* 78-2 (Eugene, Ore.: Decision Research, a Branch of Perceptronics, Inc., 1978).

79. Michael Ross and Fiore Sicoly, "Egocentric Biases in Availability and Attributions," *Journal of Personality and Social Psychology* 37 (1979): 322-336.

80. Ibid., p. 336.

81. K. R. Popper, *Conjectures and Refutations* (New York: Basic Books, 1962).

82. J. R. Platt, "Strong Inference," *Science* 146 (1964): 347-353.

83. K. R. Popper, *The Logic of Scientific Discovery* (London: Hutchinson, 1959).

84. R. Revlin and R. E. Mayer, *Human Reasoning* (New York: John Wiley, 1987).

85. B. F. Skinner, *Beyond Freedom and Dignity* (London: Basic Books, 1963).

86. P. N. Johnson-Laird and P.C. Wason (eds.), *Thinking: Reading in Cognitive Science* (New York: Cambridge University Press, 1977).

87. J. S. Evans and B. T. Evans, *The Psychology of Deductive Reasoning* (London: Rougledge and Kegan paul, 1982).

88. R. M. Dawes, "The Mind, the Model and the Task," in F. Restel, R. M. Sliffrin, N. J. Castellan, H. R. Lindman, and D. B. Risoni (eds.), *Cognitive Theory*, vol. 1 (Hillsdale, N.J.: Erlbaum, 1975); R. A. Griggs and S. E. Ravesdall, "Scientists and the Selection Task" (unpublished manuscript, Department of Psychology, University of Florida, Gainesville, 1985); R. A. Griggs and J. R. Cox, "The Elusive Thematic-Materials Effect in Wason's Selection Task," *British Journal of Psychology* 73 (1982): 407-420.

89. B. Fischhoff and R.Beyth-Maron, "hypothesis Evaluation from a Bayesian Perspective," *Psychological Review* (june 1983): 239-260; P. C. Vanduyne, "Necessity and Contingency in Reasoning," *Acta Psychologica* (May 1976): 85-101.

90. R. K. Mautz and H. A. Sharaf, *The Philosophy of Auditing*, American Accounting Association Monograph No. 6 (Evanston, Ill.: American Accounting Association, 1961).

91. Belkaoui, "Auditing and the Use of Logical Knowledge in Deductive Reasoning: An Experiment" (unpublished manuscript, University of Illinois at Chicago, 1987).

92. Joshua Klayman and young-Won Ha, "Confirmation, Disconfirmation and Information in Hypothesis Testing" (working paper, Graduate School of Business, University of Chicago, Center for Decision Research, February 1986).

93. h. R. Arkes and A. R. Harkness, "Estimates of Contingency between Two Dichotomous Variables," *Journal of Experimental Psychology* (October 1983): 117-135.

94. C. Lord, L. Ross, and M. Legger, "Biased Assimilation and Attitude Polarization: The Effect of Prior Theories on Subsequently Considered Evidence," *Journal of Personality and Social Psychology* (March 1979): 2098-2109.

95. M. Snyder, "Seek and ye Shall Find: Testing Hypotheses about Other People," in E. T. Higgins, C. P. Heiman, and M. P. Zamms (eds.), *Social Cognition: The Ontario Symposium on Personality and Social Psychology* (Hillsdale, N.J.: Erlbaum, 1981).

96. Tversky and Kahneman, "Judgment under Uncertainty," pp. 1124-1131.

97. Ibid.

98. P. Slovic, "From Shakespeare to Simon: Speculations and Some Evidence About Man's Ability to Process Information," *Research Monograph (Oregon Research Institute, April 1972).*

99. M. Albert and H. Raiffa, "A Progress Report on the Training of Probability Assessors" (unpublished manuscript, Harvard University, Graduate School of Business Administration, 1968).

100. Tversky and D. Kahneman, "Extensional versus Intuitive Reasoning: The Conjunction Fallacy in Probability judgment," *Psychological Review* (October *1983): 295.*

101. 101. Ibid., pp. 293-315.

102. Tversky, "Features of Similarity," *Psychological Review* (February 1977): 327-352.

103. H. J. Einhorn, "A Model of the Conjunction Fallacy" (working paper, Center for Decision Research, University of Chicago, June 1985).

104. Frank J. Yates and Bruce W. Carlson, "Conjunction Errors: Evidence for Multiple judgment Procedures, Including 'Signed Summation,' " *Organizational Behavior and Human Decision Processes* 37 (1986): 230-253: Dean M. Morier and Eugene Borgida, "The Conjunction Fallacy: A Task Specific Phenomenon?" *Personality and Social Psychology Bulletin* (June 1984): 243-252; john Uddo, Robert P. Abelson, and Paget H. Gross, "Conjunctive Explanations: When Two Reasons are Better Than One," *Journal of Personality and Social Psychology* (March 1984): 933-943; A. Locksley and C. Stangor, "Why vs. How Often: Causal Reasoning and Incidence of Judgmental Bias," *Journal of Experimental Social Psychology* (October 1984): 430-455.

105. B. Fischhoff, "Hindsight Foresight: The Effect of Outcome Knowledge on Judgment under Uncertainty," *Journal of Experimental Psychology: Human Perception and Performance* (May 1975): 288-299. "Perceived Informativeness of Facts," *Journal of Experimental Psychology: Human Perception and Performance* (Ma 1977): 349-358.

106. B. Fischhoff and R. Beyth, "I Knew It Would Happen: Remembered Probabilities of Once-Future Things," *Organizational Behavior and Human Performance* (February 1975): 1-16.

107. B. Fischhoff, "Debasing," in Kahneman, Slovic, and Tversky, *Judgment under Uncertainty*, p. 428.

108. Fischhoff, "Hindsight Foresight," p. 298.

109. Ibid.

110. P. Slovic and B. Fishhoff, "On the Psychology of Experimental Surprises," *Journal of Experimental Psychology: Human Perception and Performance* (November 1977): 544-551.

111. Fischhoff and Beyth, "I Knew It Would Happen."

112. Fischhoff, "Perceived Informativeness of Facts"

113. G. Wood, "The Know-It-All_Along Effect," Journal of Experimental Psychology: Human Perception and Performance (May 1978): 345-353.

114. T. Mitchell and L. Kalb, "Effects of Outcome Knowledge and Outcome Valence on Supervisors' Evaluations," *Journal of Applied Psychology* (October 1981): 604-612.

115. D. Pennington, D. Rutter, K. McKenna, and I. Morley, "Estimating the Outcome of a Pregnancy Test: Women's Judgments in Foresight and Hindsight," *British Journal of Social and Clinical Psychology* (November 1980): 317-323.

116. D. Detmer, D. Fryback, and K. Gassner, "Heuristics and Biases in Medical Decision-Making," *Journal of Medical Educations* 53 (1978): 682-683.

117. H. Arkes, R. Wortmann, P. Saville, and A. Harkness, "Hindsight Bias among Physicians Weighing the Likelihood of Diagnoses," *Journal of Applied Psychology* (October 1981): 2520254.

118. R. Hogarth, Judgment and Choice: The Psychology of Decisions (New York: John Wiley, 1980).

119. Ibid., p. 102.

120. Ibid.

121. R. Nisbett and L. Ross, *Human inference: Strategies and Shortcomings of Social Judgment* (Englewood Cliffs, N.J.: Prentice-Hall, 1980).

122. H. Einhorn and R. Hogarth, "Behavioral Decision Theory: Process of Judgment and Choice," *Journal of Accounting Research* (Spring 1981): 32-41.

123. Ross and Sicoly, "Egocentric Biases in Availability and Attribution," in Kahneman, Slovic, and Tverksy, *Judgment under Uncertainty*, pp. 179-189.

124. Hogarth, Judgment and Choice, p. 103.

125. Fischhoff, "Debasing."

126. L. J. Chapman, "Illusory Correlation in Observational Report." *Journal of Verbal Learning and Verbal Behavior* (February 1967): 151.

127. L. J. Chapman and J. P. Chapman, "Genesis of popular but Erroneous Psychodiagnostic Signs," *Journal of Abnormal Psychology* (June 1967): 193-204.

128. Ibid., p. 196.

129. L. J. Chapma and J. P. Chapman, "Illusory Correlation as an Obstacle to the Use of Valid Psychodiagnostic Signs," *Journal of Abnormal Psychology* (June 1969): 271-280.

130. S. L. Golding and L. G. Rorer, "Illusory Correlations and Subjective Judgment," *Journal of Abnormal Psychology* (June, 1978): 249-260.

131. J. Starr and E. S. Katkin. "The Clinician as an Aberrant Actuary: Illusory Correlation and the Incomplete Sentences Blank," *Journal of Abnormal Psychology* (December 1969): 670-675.

132. H. M. Jenkins and W. C. Ward, "Judgment of Contingency Between Responses and Outcomes," *Psychological Monographs:*

General and Applied, No. 594 (1965); J. Smedsbund, "The Concept of Correlation in Adults," *Scandanavian Journal of Psychology* (Third Quarter, 1963): 165-173; J. Smedsbune, "Note on Learning, Contingency, and Clinical Experience," *Scandanavian journal of Psychology* (Fourth Quarter, 1966): 265-266; W. C. Ward and H. M. Jenkins, "The Display of Information and the Judgment of Contingency," *Canadian Journal of Psychology* (September 1965): 231-241.

133. Nisbett and Ross, *Human Inference*.

134. Chapman, "Illusory Correlation in Observational Report"; Tversky and kahneman, "Availability: A Heuristic for Judging Frequency and Probability"; R. Schweder, "Likeness and Likelihood in Everyday Thought: Magical Thinking in Judgments about personality," *Current Anthropology* (December 1977): 637-658.

135. Chapman and Chapman, "Genesis of Popular but Erroneous Psychodiagnostic Observations"; "Illusory Correlation as an Obstacle to the Use of Valid Psychodiagnostic Signs."

136. Ward and Jenkins, "The Display of Information and the Judgment of Contingency"; Arkes and Harkness, "Estimates of Eontingency," pp. 117-135; H. Shaklee and M. Mins, "Sources of Error in Judging Event Covariations: Effects of Memory Demands," *Journal of Experimental Psychology: Learning, Memory and Cognition* (May 1982): 208-224.

137. J. Rose, W. Beaver, S. Becker, and G. Sorter, "Toward and Empirical Measure of Materiality," supplement to *Journal of Accounting Research* (Spring 1970): 138-148.

138. John W. Dickhaut and Ian R. C. Eggleton, "An Examination of the Processes Underlying Comparative Judgments of Numerical Stimuli," *Journal of Accounting Research* (Spring 1975): 38-72.

139. Robert P. Magee and John W. Dickhaut, "Effects of Compensation Plans on Heuristics in Cost Variance Investigations," *Journal of Accounting Research* (Autumn 1978): 294-314.

140. Robert P. Magee, "A Simulation Analysis of Alternative Cost Variance Investigation Models," *Accounting Review* (July 1976): 529-544.

141. Magee and Dickhaut, "Effects of Compensation Plans," p. 307.

BIBLIOGRAPHY

The Objective Function

Anthony, Robert N. "The Trouble with Profit Maximization." *Harvard Business Review* (November-December 1960): 126-134.

Beams, Floyd A. and Fertig, Paul E. "Pollution Control Through Social Cost Conversion." *The Journal of Accountancy* (November 1971): 37-42.

Belkaoui, Ahmed. "The Impact of the Disclosure of Environmental Effects of Organizational Behavior on the Market." *Financial management* (Winter 1976): 26-31.

Cyert, Richard M.; March, James G.: and Starbuck, William H. "Two Experiments on Bias and Conflict in Organizational Estimation." *Management Science* (April 1961): 254-264.

Donaldson, Gordon. "Financial Goals: Management Versus Stockholders." *Harvard Business Review* (May-June 1963): 116-129.

Estes, Ralph W. "Accounting for Social Costs." *The Accounting Review* (April 1972): 284-290.

Findlay, Chapman M. and Whitmore, G. A. "Beyond Shareholder Wealth maximization." *Financial management* (Winter 1974): 25-35.

Lewellen, Wilbur G. "Management and Ownership in the Large Firm." *Journal of Finance* (May 1969): 299-322.

Linowes, David F. "Socil-Economic Accounting." *The Journal of Accountancy* (November 1968): 37-42.

Livingstone, J. Leslie (ed.). *Managerial Accounting: The Behavioral Foundations.* Columbus, Ohio: Grid, 1975.

Mobley, Sybil C. "The Challenges of Socio-Economic Accounting." *The Accounting Review* (October 1970): 762-768.

Schiff, Michael, and Lewin, Arie T. "Where Traditional Budgeting Fails." *Financial Executive* (May 1968): 55-62.

Williamson, O. The Economics of Discretionary Behavior: Managerial Objectives in the Theory of the Firm. Englewood Cliffs, N.J.: Prentice-hall, 1964.

Motivation Theories

Adams, J. S. "Toward an Understanding of Inequity." *Journal of Abnormal and Social Psychology* 22 (1968): 1045-1053.

Caplan, E. H. *Management Accounting and Behavioral Science.* Reading, Mass.: Addison-Wesley, 1971.

Chung, Kae H. "Toward a General Theory of Motivation and Performance." *California Management Review* (Spring 1969): 81-88.

Herzberg, F.; Mausner, B.; and Snyderman, B. *The Motivation to Work,* 2nd ed. New York: John Wiley, 1959.

Maslow, A. "A Dynamic Theory of Human Motivation." *Psychological Review* 50 (1943): 370-373.

McClelland, D.C. *The Achieving Society.* New York: Van Nostrand, 1961.

Porter, L. W., and Lawler, E. E. *Managerial Attitudes and Performances.* Honewood, Ill.: Irwin-Dorsey, 1968.

Schein, Edgar. *Organization Psychology,* 2nd ed. Englewood Cliffs, N.J.: Prentice-Hall, 1970.

Vinacke, W. W. "Motivation as a Complex Problem." *Nebraska Symposium on Motivation.* Lincoln: University of Nebraska Press, 1962.

Vroom, V. H. *Work and Motivation.* New York: John Wiley, 1964.

Walster, E.; Berscheid, E.; and Walster, G. W. "New Directions in Equity Research." *Journal of Personality and Social Psychology* 25 (1973): 151-176.

Models of Decision Making

Allison, G. T. *Essence of a Decision.* Boston: Little, Brown, 1971.

Bariff, M. L., and Lusk, E. J. "Cognitive and Personality Tests for the Design of Management Information Systems." *Management Science* (April 1977): 820-829.

Cyert, R. M., and March, J. G. *A Behavioral Theory of the Firm.* Englewood Cliffs, N.J.: Prentice-Hall, 1963.

Dermer, J. "Cognitive Characteristics and the Perceived Importance of Information." *The Accounting Review* (January 1973): 511-519.

Goldstein, Kenneth, and Blackman, Sheldon. *Cognitive Style: Five Approaches and Relevant Research.* New York: John Wiley, 1978.

Huysmans, Jan H. B. "The Effectiveness of the Cognitive-Style Constraint in Implementing Operations Research Proposals." *Management Science* (September 1970): 92-104.

Keen, Peter G., and Scott Morton, Michael S. *Decision Support Systems: An Organizational Perspective.* Addison-Wesley Series on Decision Support. Reading, Mass.: Addison-Wesley, 1978.

Lindblom, C. W. "The Science of Muddling Through." *Public Administrative Review* (Spring 1959): 79-88.

March, J. G., and Simon, H. A. *Organizations.* New York: John Wiley, 1958.

Schroder, H. M.; Driver, M. J.; and Streufert, S. *Human Information Processing.* New York: Holt, Rinehart and Winston, 1967.

Simon, Herbert A. *Administrative Behavior,* 2nd ed. New York: Macmillan, 1957.

Sorter, George H., Becker, Selwyn W.; Archibald, T. R.; and Beaver, W. "Corporate Personality as Reflected in Accounting Decisions: Some Preliminary Findings." *Journal of Accounting Research* (Autumn 1964): 183-196.

Heuristics and Biases

Belkaoui, A. "Auditing and the Use of Logical Knowledge in Deductive Reasoning: An Experiment." Unpublished Manuscript, University of Illinois at Chicago, 1987.

Belkaoui, A. *Human Information Processing in Accounting.* Westport, CT: Quorum Books, 1989.

Brichman, Thomas A. "An Effect of Hindsight on Predicting Bankruptcy with Accounting Information." *Accounting, Organizations and Society* (August 1988): 267-285.

Brown, Clifton E., and Solomon, Ira. "Effects of Outcome Information on Evaluations of Managerial Decision." *Accounting Review* (July 1987): 564-577.

Dickhaut, John W., and Eggleton, Ian R. C. "An Examination of the Processes Underlying Comparative Judgments of Numerical Stimuli." *Journal of Accounting Research* (Spring 1975): 38-72.

Frederick, David M., and Libby, Robert. "Expertise and Auditors' Judgments of Conjunctive Events." *Journal of Accounting Research* (Autumn 1986): 270-290.

Givvins, M. "Human Inference, Heuristics and Auditors' Judgment Processes." In *CICA Auditing Research Symposium.* Toronto: Canadian Institute of Certified Public Accountants (CICA), 1977.

Johnson, W. Bruce. "'Representativeness' in Judgmental Predictions of Corporate Bankruptcy." *Accounting Review* (January 1983): 78-97.

Joyce, Edward J., and Biddle, Gary C. "Anchoring and Adjustment in Probabilistic Inference in Auditing." *Journal of Accounting Research* (Spring 1981): 120-145.

———. "Are Auditors' Judgments Sufficiently Regressive?" *Journal of Accounting Research* (Autumn 1981): 323-349.

Magee, Robert P. "A Simulation Analysis of Alternative Cost Variance Investigation Models." *Accounting Review* (July 1976): 529-544.

Magee, Rober P., and Dickhaut, John W. "Effects of Compensation Plans on Heuristics in Cost Variance Investigations." *Journal of Accounting Research* (Autumn 1978): 294-314.

Rose, J.; Beaver, W.; Becker, S.;; and Sorter, G. "Toward an Empirical

Measure of Materiality." Supplement to *Journal of Accounting Research* (Spring 1975): 38-72.

Swieringa, Robert; Gibbins, Michael; Larson, Lars; and Lawson Sweeny, Janet. "Experiments in the Heuristics of Human Information Processing." Supplement to *Journal of Accounting Research* (1976): 159-187.

4. COGNITIVE RELATIVISM IN INFORMATION MANAGEMENT

What happens when people make decisions about an business phenomenon, amid the pressures, constraints, dangers, and opportunities of today's business environment?[1] This chapter presents a model which focuses on the cognitive processes employed by a decision maker attempting to use his/her judgment to make a decision about a business phenomenon. Basically, both judgment and decision are the products of a set of social cognitive operations that include the observation of information on the business phenomenon and the formation of a schema to represent the business phenomenon that is stored in memory and later retrieved when needed to allow the formation of a judgment and a decision. Before presenting the model an elaboration on the notion and use of schemata in cognitive psychology and accounting is necessary.

SCHEMATA IN COGNITIVE PSYCHOLOGY

The Notion of Schema-Guided Processes

The schema theory as developed by F.C. Barlett[2] served as the stimulus for all schema theories. As defined by Barlett, a schema is "an active organization of past reactions, or past experiences, which must always be supposed to be operating in any well-adapted organic response."[3] They are complex unconscious knowledge, as "masses of organized past experiences."[4] They are generic cognitive representations, in the sense that they constitute a process that can deal with an indefinitely large number of new instances.

Modern views of schemata refer generally to cognitive structures that represent organized knowledge about a given concept or a given stimulus and that serve as mechanisms for the interaction of old knowledge and new knowledge in perception, language, thought, and memory.

Schemata are generally regarded as fundamental elements upon which all information processing depends. They constitute a theory about knowledge: how knowledge is represented, and how that representation facilitates the use of knowledge in numerous ways. As stated by D. E. Rumelhart, "schemata are employed in the process of interpreting sensory data, in retrieving information from memory, in organizing actions, in the determining of goals and sub-goals, in the allocation of resources and generally in guiding the flow of processing in the system."[5] In fact, useful analyses of schemata suggested by Rumelhart include plays, theories, procedures, and parsers.[6] Properties of schemas include the following:

1. A schema represents a prototypical abstraction of the complex concept it represents.

2. A schema is induced from past experiences with numerous exemplars of the complex concept it represents.

3. A schema can guide the organization of incoming information into clusters of knowledge that are "instantiations" of the schema itself.

4. When one of the constituent concepts of a schema is missing in the input, its features can be inferred from default values" in the schema.[7]

Schemata versus Categories

Jean Randler made an unusual distinction between two types of representations— categories and schemata. Categories are denoted by verbal or nonverbal symbols (i.e., "names") and are represented by a set of features that serve as the basis for inferring membership in it. Schemata, on the other hand, are cognitive representations whose features, like those of categories, are organized according to specific a priori spatial, temporal, or logical criteria.[8] Categories and schemata function differently. As Robert S. Wyer and S.E. Gordon note:

> Information about a set of attributes processed by the members of a particular category may not spontaneously activate this category unless either (a) the attributes are very strongly and uniquely associated with it, (b) one has a specific objective that leads the object being described

> to be classified, or (c) a category and its characteristic features are already activated at the time the information is received... In contrast, information that describes the characteristic features of a schema may become more inclined to activate the schema spontaneously.[9]

Schema Growth and Change

In considering schema growth and change the evidence favors a perseverance effect whereby generic schemata are resistant to change even in the face of contrary evidence.[10] In fact, people may even interpret exceptions as proving a given schema,[11] unless they are asked to counter argue it, to explain why their favorite theory might be wrong.[12]

Schemata are developed from experience with instances of the category in question and become more complex, more abstract, and more organized with experience. With increasing experience a schema becomes more mature and more complex. Hence, the schemata of experts contain more informational elements than those of novices, are more organized, contain more links, and may have a more complex hierarchy.[13-15]

Sources of Activation for Schemas

D.G. Bobrow and D.A. Norman distinguish between two basic sources of activation for schemata: conceptually driven and data-driven processing.[16] In conceptually driven processing, an activated schema in turn activates a subschemata with the expectation that this will account for some portion of the input data. In data-driven processing, the activated subschema causes the activation of the various schemas of which it is a component. Data-driven processing goes from part to the whole. In another source of activation, known as schema-directed processing, the activation is assumed to go in both directions. It proceeds as follows:

> Some events occur at the sensory system. The occurrence of this event "automatically activates certain low level" schemata (much schemata might be called "*feature detectors*"). The low level schemata, in turn, activates (in a data driven fashion) certain of the "higher level" schemata (the most probable ones) of which they are constituents. These "higher level" schemata then initiate conceptually driven processing by activating the subschemata not already activated in an attempt to evaluate their goodness of fit.[17]

Encoding of Information in a Schema

For W.F. Brewer and G.V. Nakamura, the interaction of old knowledge with new knowledge involves two processes: one refers to the modification of the generic knowledge in the relevant schema, while the other refers to the construction of a specified instantiated memory representation, where the instantiated schema is the cognitive structure that results from the interaction of the old information and the new information from the episodic unit.[18]

The encoding of information is in fact subject to at least two interpretations. First, the interpretation proposed by R. S.

Woodswork and H. Schlosberg[19] postulates that once a schema is activated by incoming episodic information, features that are inconsistent with the implications of this schema are appended to the representation of information as "corrections." A second conceptualization proposed by A. C. Graesser, S.E. Gordon, and J.D. Sawyer,[20] known as the "script-pointer-plus-tag formulation, postulates that when people receive information that is interpretable in terms of a prototypic event schema (script), they do not retain the information itself but a "pointer" to the general script, along with an indication of the values of the information that instantiate the script variables. If features of the information do not match attributes of the generic script, and thus cannot be reconstructed, they are appended to the representations as "tag." Basically, new information is represented by a series of "pointer" to prototypic event schemata that can be used to understand or describe the event, accompanied when necessary by "tags" denoting objects or events that cannot be derived from the event schemata alone.

Social Schema Research

Social schema research investigates self-schemata, person schemata, script or event schemata, and person-in-situation schemata.[21]

The self-schema contains cognitive generalizations about the self that are derived from past experiences. People are generally self-schematic on dimensions that are of importance to them, on which they perceive themselves as extreme, and on which they perceive the opposite to be untrue.[22] They are schematic on those dimensions perceived to be of lesser importance to them.

Research on perception shows that people who are schematic on a particular dimension recognize and filter rapidly incoming information about the dimension, notice the dimension in other people, and think harder about kinds of schema-relevant information.[23]

Research on memory shows that self-schematic people remember shema-relevant information, are difficult to change, have more accessible knowledge about others because of the sheer familiarity of self-knowledge, and are more affect-laden in knowledge about others, especially unfamiliar individuals.[24,25]

Research on inference shows that people make rapid predictions about their own behavior that are consistent with their self-schemata.[26] Under certain circumstances these predictions take longer than for aschematics,[27] especially if the judgment is novel.

The person-schema contains cognitive generalizations about trait and behavior information common to certain groups or types of people.

Research on perception shows that categories for people, like categories for objects, are organized hierarchically.[28] Research on memory shows that schemata for people's traits and goals typically help the perceiver to remember schema-consistent information in more detail than would be possible without the schemata. Research on inference shows that person schemata affect subsequent inferences.

The evidence on person schemata is summarized as follows:

> Person schemata include protypical representations of traits such as extroversion and introversion, as well as

> notions of what behavior is consistent with a given goal. Person schemata of all sorts shape the processes of perception, memory, and inference to conform to our general assumptions about other people. The effects of schemata on perception, memory and inference are not necessarily well suited to accuracy in identifying individual instances. Schemata are used by the mind to manage such processes economically, if not accurately.[29]

The script or event schema contains cognitive generalizations that describe the appropriate sequence of events in a given situation.[30] Research on script or event schemata is summarized as follows:

> Script or event schema describe sequences of activity from everyday life. They contain props, roles and sequence rules. Scripts also may be subjivided into segments (scenes). Like other schemata, scripts guide the perception of ambiguous information and often shape memory toward schema consistent information. Inferences can be seen as filling in gaps where information was missing, and gap filling appears to be exaggerated by repeated encounters with the script. Most of the functions of scripts echo those of other schemata, in their focus on relevant—and usually on consistent—information in perception, memory and inference.[31]

The person-in-situation or role schema contains cognitive generalizations about people in situations or scripts for behavior in situations. Role schemata not only help perception, memory, and inference but may be a way to account for stereotyping.

Research on perception shows that categorization instantiates the stereotypic content of the schema whether or not the person fits the category and in the process minimizes the amount of variability and complexity that may exist in the category.[32,33] In addition to minimizing variability and complexity, a schema slants perception of the content of what a person does.

Research on memory shows that the role schema shapes memory in a schema-consistent fashion. In addition, the categorical information seems to override the details of the specific instance.[34] Schema-discrepant information is, however, likely to receive added attention at input, if task conditions allow. Attentional processes can facilitate remembering inconsistent information.[35]

SCHEMA-BASED RESEARCH IN ACCOUNTING

Cognitive Research in Information Management

The cognitive revolution in social psychology has created strong interest in the knowledge structure in memory in general and how people learn in particular. This research paradigm also affects accounting and auditing. Given that the difference between declarative knowledge and procedural knowledge is equivalent to the difference between content knowledge and the use of that knowledge or between "knowing what" and "knowing how," W.S. Waller and W.L. Felix used the concepts to propose a model of how an ordinary person learns from experience.[36] Basically,

> Its thesis is that learning from experience involves the formation and development of generalized cognitive structures that organize experience-based declarative and procedural knowledge in long term memory. Declarative knowledge is organized by categories, which depend on similarity of class membership relations, and schemata, which depend on spatial and/or temporal relations. Procedural knowledge is organized into production systems, i.e., hierarchies of condition-action pairs.[37]

What the model implies is that schemata are developed through a gradual process of abstracting domain-specific knowledge on the basis of experience. The difference between the expert and the novice's knowledge structure is therefore the result of difference in experience. What is apparent from the research on novices and experts is that longer chunks of information are taken and stored by experts than novices at any point in time and for a particular task;[38,39] pieces of information are better clustered into meaningful categories within a single chunk by experts;[40] and the recall of experts is based on conceptual representations for information while the novices' is based on functional relationships.[41-44]

The findings in accounting so far parallel those in psychology. More specifically, R. Weber found that expert auditors clustered internal control cues according to their control categories significantly more than novices did.[45] D.M. Frederick and R. Libby found that expert auditors clustered financial statement errors by transaction cycles.[46]

Propositions about Knowledge Structures in Information Management

The notion of schemas (knowledge structures or templates) was used by Michael Gibbins to make general propositions, corollaries, and hypotheses about the psychological operations of professional judgment in the "natural" everyday settings experienced by public accountants.[47] Professional judgment in public accounting was described as a five-component process:

- Schemas or knowledge structures accumulated through learning or experience
- A triggering event or stimulus
- A judgment environment
- A judgment process
- A decision/action

The list of propositions, corollaries, and hypotheses is shown in Exhibit 4.1. While it awaits empirical validation, the list constitutes one general descriptive theory of professional judgment in public accounting, where auditor judgment is viewed as a responsive, continuous, unconscious, instrumental process of sequentially matching cues to knowledge structures to generate preferences and responses based on experience.[48] Preliminary findings on these propositions are provided by Gibbins,[49] Gibbins and Emby,[50] and Emby and Gibbins.[51]

Exhibit 4.1

List of Propositions and Corollaries

A. Propositions about the routine PJPA cycle

A(1). The judge's experience (accumulated learning)

P1. Experience produces structured judgment guides ("templates")

C1(i): Template exists prior to event triggering its use

C1(ii): Greater experience, more efficient memory use

C1(iii): Template more complete for more common tasks

P2: The templates are maintained in long-term memory

P3: Templates' attributes are shaped by the environment

C3(i): Some templates more ready for use than others

A(2). The triggering event (stimulus)

P4: The environment is subjectively perceived

C4(i): Factors limiting perception also limit judgment

P5: Templates are continuously updated

A(3). The judgment process

P6: Judgment is a continuous process

P7: Judgment is an incremental process

C7(i): Routine judgment responds to the short term

C7(ii): Routine judgment avoids limits on future responses

P8: Judgment is a conditional process

P9: Judgment begins with a search for a template

C9(i): Search-retrieval may use little information

P10: Template selection depends on circumstantial fit

C10(i): Routine templates selection based on past learning

C10(ii): Perception and search continue until template found

P11: Routine judgment is not, and need not be, conscious

C11(i): Explaining own judgment involves rationalization

C11(ii): Own explanations correlate with common templates

P12: The judgment environment is incompletely perceived

P13: Personal characteristics affect template selection

A(4). The decision/action (response)

P14: Templates specify conscious response preferences

Exhibit 1.1 (continued)

C14(i): As outputs, preferences subject to imperfections

C14(ii): Preferences based on past actions and learning

P15: Preferences and actions are consciously bridged

P16: The bridging process is instrumental, not probabilistic

C16(i): Preferences, consequences instrumentally connected

P17: The decision/action must be justifiable

C17(i): Some information is to justify choice, not make it

C17(ii): Justification includes some rationalization

P18: Bridging evaluations tend to emphasize the downside

B. Propositions about nonroutine PJPA

P19: Conscious judgment is a response to the circumstances

P20: Conscious judgment strategies also guide judgment

C20(i): Mental "red flags" prompt conscious intervention

C20(ii): Complex responses need conscious implementation

P21: Fully conscious professional judgment is infrequent

Source: Michael Gibbins, "Propositions about the Psychology of Professional Judgment in Public Accounting." *Journal of Accounting Research* (Spring 1984): 121. Reprinted with permission.

A CONGNITIVE VIEW OF THE JUDGMENT/DECISION PROCESS IN INFORMATION MANAGEMENT

In what follows a model of the judgment/decision process in information management is proposed as an exercise in social perception and cognition, requiring both formal and implicit judgment.[52] The primary input to this process is an business problem or phenomenon that needs to be solved and requires a judgment preceding either a preference or a decision. The model consists of the following steps:

1. Observation of the business phenomenon by the decision maker
2. Schema formation or building of the business phenomenon
3. Schema organization or storage
4. Attention and recognition process triggered by a stimulus
5. Retrieval of stored information needed for the judgment decision
6. Reconsideration and integration of retrieved information with new information
7. Judgment process
8. Decision/action response

Observation of the Business Phenomenon by the Decision Maker

The decision maker is assumed to have the opportunity to observe the business phenomenon. To understand the business phenomenon, the decision maker may be given some information which is deemed diagnostic. If this information is not provided, the decision maker may seek the information and test available information judged most relevant to the phenomenon. Following H.H. Kelly's approach to causal attribution,[53] the search behavior may concentrate on these types of available information:

1. *Consensus information:* how this accounting phenomenon and other accounting phenomena were rated or performed on given dimensions
2. *Distinctiveness information:* how this accounting phenomenon was rated or performed on various other dimensions
3. *Consistency information:* how this accounting phenomenon was rated or performed on important dimensions in the past

Evidence shows that subjects tend to focus more on distinctiveness or consistency information than on consensus information.[54] Studies examining search behavior in reaction to an accounting phenomenon are very limited.

The search behavior is not misguided. It is fair to assume that the decision maker has some expectations about the accounting phenomenon which may determine the type of information sought. These expectations are termed *preconceived notions* in A. S. De Nisi et al.'s model.[55] They result from the decision maker's previous experiences with the accounting phenomenon. These expectations or preconceived notions may bias the decision maker toward choosing some information rather than other information. Providing background information prior to observation contributes to this phenomenon.[56,57] R. S. Wyer and T. K. Srull maintain that prior information predisposes the subject to select one of a number of frames of references.[58] Bias is a result of the tendency to seek evidence confirming preconceived notions rather than neutral or disconfirming evidence.[59-61]

Schema Formation or Building

Once the business phenomenon has been observed, the relevant information is encoded in the sense that it is categorized on the basis of experience and organized in memory along schemata or knowledge structures. As put by R. E. Nisbett and L. Ross:

> Few, if any, stimuli are approached for the first time by the adult. Instead, they are processed through pre-existing systems of schematized and abstracted knowledge-beliefs, theories, propositions and schemas. These knowledge structures label and categorized objects and events quickly and, for the most part, accurately.

> They also define a set of expectations about objects and events and suggest appropriate responses to them.[62]

A schema can be simply an update of templates that existed prior to the occurrence of a known business phenomenon or a new template generated by the occurrence of a new business phenomenon. In the first case, little ambiguity is assumed to exist and therefore the encoding follows an automatic process.[63] In the second case, no immediate available schema exists, and a controlled categorization process is triggered to determine which schema is consistent with the dimensions of the accounting phenomenon. Both processes are suggested in the case of the encoding of information or performance appraisal:

> Thus, both the automatic and controlled processes have the same end result: the assignment of a person to a category based on prototype-matching process. The difference is whether the stimulus person's behavior is sufficiently consistent with other cues to allow the categorization to proceed automatically or whether a controlled process must be used to determine which category is consistent with the individual's behavior. The actual category assignment is a function of contextual factors influencing the salience of particular categories and stimulus characteristics, as well as individual differences among perceivers that render some categories and their prototypes more available than others and some stimulus features more salient than others.[64]

Basically, a business phenomenon may be categorized in a given schema, by virtue of its possession of obvious or salient attributes known to the perceiver. When no salient category prototype or schema provides a natural framework, the automatic process is superseded by a controlled process or a consciously monitored process.[65]

The controlled process can be triggered by either a new business phenomenon or new features of a known phenomenon that are inconsistent with a previous categorization. In the latter case a recategorization is invoked until the inconsistency is resolved and a new schema is used to describe the business phenomenon, causing a reconstruction of memories about the phenomenon such that memories consistent with the new categorization are more available.

Schema Organization and Storage

After information about a given phenomenon is encoded to form a representation or schema, it is stored and maintained in long-term memory. E. Tulving distinguishes between episodic and semantic memory.[66] Basically, a person's episodic memories are personal while semantic memory is knowledge of words and symbols, their meanings and referent knowledge of the relations among words, and the rules or algorithms for manipulating words, symbols and the relations among them. R. C. Atkinson and R. M. Shiffrin maintain that the basic structural features of episodic memory are three memory stores: the sensory register, the short-term store, and the long-term store.[67] Information enters the memory system through the various senses and goes first to the sensory register whose function is to preserve incoming information long enough for it to be selectively transmitted into the memory system. It is kept there less than a second and is lost either through decay or erasure by overwriting.

The information then goes to the short-term store, "working in memory" where conscious mental processes are performed. It is where consciousness exercises its function. Information can be kept indefinitely here provided that it is given constant attention; if not, it is lost through decay in twenty to thirty seconds.

The information next goes to the long-term store through a conscious or unconscious process where it can be held indefinitely and often permanently (although it can be lost due to decay or interference of various sorts). The long-term store is assumed to have unlimited capacity. In this multistore model information about the business phenomenon moves through different and separate memory systems, ending with a long-term store where semantic information is maintained along meaning-based codes or schemata. It is important to realize at this stage that if the person intends to remember the business phenomenon for all time, he/she must perform a different analysis on the input than when his/her intentions are temporary.[68] A person's intention determines whether the storage of the information on the business phenomenon is permanent or temporary. A different coding is used: a memory code for permanent storage and a perceptual role for temporary storage.

> Different codes have different permanence. Codes of the sensory aspects of an input, such as appearance, are short lived. Hence, a person who looked at a word to decide whether it was printed in red or green would

> not remember the word's name very long because his coding would have emphasized color, not meaning. In contrast, a person who looked at a word to decide whether it was a synonym for some other word would form a semantic code, and he/she would remember the name of the examined word for quite a while.[69]

Stimulus and Attention and Recognition Processes

Upon observation of a triggering event or stimulus, the schema in the accounting phenomenon is activated. The activation, as a process of detection, search, and attention, can be either a controlled or an automatic processing.[70]

Basically, automatic detection, triggered by the recognition of a stimulus, operates independently of the person's control. Automatic processing is the apprehension of stimuli by the use of previously learned routines that are in the long-term storage.

> Automatic processing as learned in long-term store, is triggered by appropriate inputs, and then operates independently of the subject's control. An automatic sequence can contain components that control information flow, attract attention, or govern overt responses. Automatic sequences do not require attention, though they may attract it if training is appropriate, and they do not use up short-term capacity. They are learned following the earlier use of controlled processing that links the same nodes in sequence. In search, detection,

> and attention tasks, automatic detection develops when stimuli are consistently mapped to responses; then the targets develop the ability to attract attention and initiate responses automatically, immediately, and regardless of other inputs or memory load.[71]

In these automatic processes, no conscious effort is involved in the search as well as in demanding attention due to the learned sequence of the elements composing the schemata. On the other hand, controlled processes involve a temporary activation of novel sequences of processing steps that require attention, use short-term memory, and involve a conscious effort.

It is important to realize that in both processes, the use of schemata for encoding or retrieving information depends on accessibility in memory, where the accessibility of schemata is the probability that they can be activated, either for use in storage of incoming information or for retrieval of previously stored information.[72,73]

> Accessibility of a schema depends upon such factors as the strength of the stored information, the extent of the overlap or match between input and schema, and the recency and frequency of previous activations. Each time a schema is activated for use, it becomes more accessible for successive activations. The instrumental effect of an activation on the accessibility of a schema is presumably a decreasing function of its prior strength.

That is, a weak schema benefits more from an activation than a strong one.[74]

Empirical evidence on the increased accessibility of information with the frequency of activation is available.[75,76]

Retrieval of Stored Information Needed for Judgment/Decision

Either the automatic or controlled search processes activate the appropriate schema for the business phenomenon and allow the retrieval of information on the phenomenon. It is, however, the schema, a representation of the phenomenon, that is recalled rather than the actual phenomenon.[77-79] The effect becomes stronger as the time between observation and recall increases.[80]

The potential for different types of biases exists at this stage. For example, people may be more likely to recall information consistent with a schema confirming an expectation,[81] or may recall schema-consistent information which they never saw.[82] A good deal of evidence also suggests that schema-inconsistent information is more likely to be recalled[83] because of its novelty, saliency, and difficulty of incorporation into a schema.[84]

What is more likely to be recalled when faced with a business phenomenon, what types of biases affect the recall of schemata of accounting phenomena, and what can be done to reduce or eliminate the distortions in recall are some of the important questions in need of investigation. This model will assume that familiarity with the business phenomenon through constant record keeping and other forms of monitoring may result in less biased recall. The solution, in fact, is more complex and depends on the type of relationship between memory and judgment. Reid Hastie and Bernadette Park investigated these relationships and distinguished between two types of judgment tasks, memory-based and on-line. They also identified five information-processing models that relate memory for evidence to judgment based on the evidence: (1) independent processing, (2) availability, (3) biased retrieval, (4) biased encoding, and (5) incongruity-biased encoding.[85]

With regard to the five information-processing models, the distinction is threefold: (1) cases where there is no relation between judgment and memory processes which include the independent processing model; (2) cases where memory availability causes judgment which include the availability-based information-processing model and the automatic search process described earlier; and (3) cases where judgment causes memory which include the biased retrieval, the biased encoding, and incongruity-biased encoding models. The biased retrieval model is selective in the sense that traces which "fit" the judgment are more likely to be found at the memory decision stage. Such biases have been termed *selective recall, confirmatory memory,* and *access-biased memory.*[86-89]

The biased encoding model assumes that biasing takes place at the time of the encoding of evidence information and memory search will locate a biased sample of information reflecting the initial encoding bias.

The incongruity-based encoding model assumes after the initial encoding, incoming information that is incongruent or contradictory is given special processing to enhance its memorability by being placed in "special tags" that strongly attach to memory. In memory search, the subject is more likely to find the incongruent information.[90,91]

This model assumes that where the business phenomenon calls for an online task, the availability or automatic search model will characterize the retrieval of stored information needed for judgment decision. Selection of a processing model will depend on the individual objectives of the subject and the perceived consequences of his/her judgments on his/her economic and psychological welfare.

Reconsideration and Integration of Retrieved Information with Other Available Information

At this stage the process involves the integration of the information retrieved from memory and other available information into a single evaluation of the business phenomenon.

Where familiarity with the phenomenon is present and previously learned routines are retrieved active integration will not take place. An earlier integration is recalled from past stored output on the phenomenon. "What was once accomplished by slow, conscious, deductive reasoning is now arrived at by fast, unconscious perceptual processing."[92]

Where the phenomenon presents challenging and novel dimensions and where controlled processes were involved in attention and recognition, a cognitive integration of all the information is required to reach a single evaludation of the business phenomenon. G. Mandler describes the process of "response learning" as follows:

> First, the organism makes a series of discrete responses, often interrupted by incorrect ones. However, once errors are dropped out and the sequence of behavior becomes relatively stable—as in running a maze, speaking a word, reproducing a visual pattern—the various components of the total behavior required in the situation are "integrated." Integration refers to the face that previously discrete parts of a sequence come to behave functionally as a unit; the whole sequence is elicited as a unit and behaves as a single component response has in the past; any part of it elicits the whole sequence.[93]

Brunswick's lens model and Anderson's weighted average model provide support to the types of integration of information that take place.[94] The integration process is, however, also subject to various biases:

1. People may attach and give great weight to some type of information. For example, evidence in the employee appraisal literature shows that negative information has greater weight.[95,96]

2. There is evidence in both psychology and accounting of an underutilization or underweighing of base rate or consensus information.[97]

3. There is ample evidence in psychology and accounting of the effect of various heuristics involved in decisions on and about accounting phenomena. They include (1) representativeness, (2) availability, (3) confirmation bias, (4) anchoring and adjustment, (5) conjunction fallacy, (6) hindsight bias, (7) illusory correlation and contingency judgments, (8) selective perception, (9) frequency, (10) concrete information, (11) data presentation, (12) inconsistency, (13) conservation, (14) nonlinear extrapolation, (15) law of small numbers, (16) habit/"rules of thumb," (17) "best-guess" strategy, (18) complexity in the decision environment, (19) social pressures in the decision environment, (20) consistency of information sources, (21) question format, (22) scale effects, (23) wishful thinking, (24) outcome-irrelevant learning structures, (25) misperceptions of chance fluctuations (Gambler's fallacy), (26) success/failure attributions, and (27) logical fallacies in recall.[98]

The Judgment Process

The judgment process is the result of the integration process of information and the forming of a single evaluation of the business phenomenon if the attention, recognition, and integration processes are the result of controlled processes. The judgment made in this case requires a conscious access to all the mental processes implied in the model. If, however, the attention, retrieval recognition, and integration processes were the result of automatic processes, the judgment is not and will not be conscious. It does not require the conscious use of all the mental processes implied in this model.[99,100] It is a routine judgment.

> Routine judgment involves the rapid matching of immediate perceptions to a template which provides, and executes, a specific response, "if total debts do not equal total credits, re-add the total balance."
>
> In the above example, there is no awareness of how the brain actually decides that the debits do not equal the credits. Even if awareness were possible, it is not normally necessary—a great many of our routine activities, such as keeping our eyes open or holding our pencils, are done without any particular conscious awareness, at least until something causes us to become aware.[101]

Decision/Action (Response)

The final step of the model is the decision or selection of a response to the business phenomenon. It is a conscious response preference resulting from the judgment process. It is an output of the judgment process and is clearly influenced by all the mental processes and biases described earlier. As a result, a new schema on the phenomenon will develop that will be part of the knowledge structure or the phenomenon stored in long-term memory.

The move from judgment to decision is a bridging process. It assumes that no obstacles stand in the way.

The decision/action has been investigated in various business environments and using various business phenomena. It has been found to differ from various normative decision models, including Bayerian-decision theory and expected value models.[102,103]

The bridging process, however, will be influenced by the cognitive steps described in this model as well as by other factors including the possible consequences of the decision on the business phenomenon. Gibbins, for instances, cites the following factors:

> Personal attitudes may play a direct role, much as determining priorities within the search process. For example, some public accountants may use financial return as their first selection criterion; others may use moral propriety as their first. Personal attitudes can also play an indirect role, limiting past actions and thus limiting the experiences on which judgment guides are built. The applications of such attitudes to the judgment process need not be conscious—particularly for deeply ingrained beliefs.[104]

CONCLUSIONS

The essence of cognitive relativism in information management is the presence of a cognitive process that is assumed to guide the judgment/decision process. The model in this chapter shows that judgments and decisions made about business and information phenomena are the products of a set of social cognitive operations that include the observation of information on accounting phenomena and the formation of schemata that are stored in memory and later retrieved to allow the formation of judgments and/or decisions when needed.

NOTES

1. W. I. Felix, Jr., and W. R. Kinney, Jr., "Research in the Auditor's Opinion Formulation Process: State of the Art," *Accounting Review* (Apr. 1988): 245-71.

2. F.C. Bartlett, *Remembering* (London: Cambridge University Press, 1932).

3. Ibid., 201.

4. Ibid, 197-98.

5. D. E. Rumelhart, "Schemata and the Cognitive System," in R. S. Wyer, Jr., and T.K. Srull, eds., *Handbook of Social Cognition* (Hillsdale, N.J.: Erlbaum, 1984), 1:162.

6. Ibid.

7. Perry W. Thorndyke and B. Hayes-Roth, "The Use of Schemata in the Acquisition and Transfer of Knowledge," *Cognitive Psychology* 11 (1979): 83.

8. Jean Mandler, "Categorical and Schematic Organization in Memory," in R. C. Ruff, *Memory, Organization and Structure* (New York: Academic Press, 1979).

9. Robert S. Wyer, Jr., and S.E. Gordon, "The Cognitive Representation of Social Information," in R.S. Wyer, Jr., and T.K. Srull, eds., *Handbook of Social Cognition* (Hillsdale, N.J.: Erlbaum, 1984), 2:82.

10. L. Ross, M. R. Lepper, and M. Hubbard, "Perseverance in Self-Perception and Social Perception: Biased Attribution Processes in the Debriefing Paradigm," *Journal of Personality and Social Psychology* 32 (1975): 880-92.

11. C. A. Anderson, "Inoculation and Counter-Explanation: Debasing Techniques in the Perseverance of Social Theories," *Social Cognition* 1 (1982): 126-35.

12. W. G. Chase and H. A. Simon, "The Mind's Eye in Chess," in W. G. Chase, ed., *Visual Information Processing* (New York: Academic Press, 1982).

13. M. T. H. Chi and R. Koeske, "Network Representations of a Child's Dinosaur Knowledge," *Developmental Psychology* 19 (1983):29-35.

14. J. H. Larkin, et al., "Models of Competence in Solving Physics Problems," *Science* 200 (1980): 1335-42.

15. K. B. McKeithen, et al., "Knowledge Organization and Skill Differences in Computer Programmers, *Cognitive Psychology* 13 (1981): 307-25.

16. D. G. Bobrow and D. A. Norman, "Some Principles of Memory Schemata," in D. G. Bobrow and A. M. Collins, eds., *Representations and Understanding: Studies in Cognitive Science* (New York: Academic Press, 1975): 25-32.

17. D. E. Rumelhart, " Schemata and the Cognitive System," in R. S. Wyer, Jr., and T. K. Srull, *Handbook of Social Cognition* (Hillsdale, N. J.: Erlbaum, 1984), 1:170.

18. W. F. Brewer and G. V. Nalsamura, " The Nature and Functions of Schemas," in R. S. Wyer, Jr. and T. K. Srull, *Handbook of Social Cognition,* (Hillsdale, N.J.: Erlbaum, 1984), 1:141.

19. R. S. Woodswork and H. Schlosberg, *Experimental Psychology* (New York: Holt, 1954).

20. C. Graesser, S. E. Gordon, and J. D. Sawyer, "Memory for Typical and Atypical Actions in Script Activities: Test of a Script Pointer + Tag Hypothesis," *Journal of Verbal Learning and Behavior* 18 (1979):503-15.

21. S. E. Taylor, and J. Crocker, "Schematic Bases of Social Information Processing," in E. T. Higgins, C. P. Herman, and M. P. Zanna, eds., *Social Cognition: The Ontario Symposium,* vol. 1 (Hillsdale, N.J.: Erlbaum, 1981).

22. H.Markus, "Self-Schemata and Processing Information about the Self," *Journal of Personality and Social Psychology* 38 (1980):231-48.

23. H. Markus, and K. P. Sentis, "The Self in Social Information Processing," in J. Suls, ed., *Psychological Perspectives on the Self,* vol. 1 (Hillsdale, N.J.: Erlbaum, 1982).

24. J. A. Bargh, "Attention and Automaticity in the Processing of Self-Relevant Information," *Journal of Personality and Social Psychology* 43 (1982):425-36.

25. T. J. Ferguson, B. G. Rule, and D. Carlson, "Memory for Personally Relevant Information." *Journal of Personality and Social Psychology* 44 (1983):251-61.

26. H. Rankus, "Self-Schema DNA Processing Information about the Self," *Journal of Personality and Social Psychology* 35 (1977):63-78.

27. N. A. Kuiper, "Convergent Evidence for the Self as a Prototype," *Personality and Social Psychology Bulletin* 7 (1981); 438-43.

28. N. Canton and . Mischel, "Prototypes in Person Perception," in L. Berkowitz, ed., *Advances in Experimental Psychology,* vol. 12 (New York: Academic Press, 1979).

29. S. T. Fiske and S. E. Taylor, *Social Cognition* (New York: Random House, 1984), 154.

30. R. P. Abelson, "The Psychological Status of the Script Concept," *American Psychologist* 36 (1981):715-25.

31. Fiske and Taylor, *Social Cognition,* 169.

32. R. S. Malpass, H. Lavingnern, and D. E. Weldon, "Verbal and Visual Training in Face Recognition," *Perception and Psychophysics* 14 (1973): 285-92.

33. P. W. Linville and E. E. Jones, "Polonized Appraisals of Outgroup Members," *Journal of Personality and Social Psychology* 42 (1982): 193-211.

34. S. E. Taylor, et al., "Categorical Bases of Person Memory and Stereotyping," *Journal of Personality and Social Psychology* 36 (1978): 778-93.

35. R. Hastie, "Memory for Behavioral Information That Confirms or Contradicts a Personality Impression," in R. Hastie, et al., eds., *Person Memory: The Cognitive Basis of Social Perception* (Hillsdale, N.J.: Erlbaum, 1981).

36. W. S. Waller and W. L. Felix, Jr., "The Auditor and Learning from Experience: Some Conjectures," *Accounting, Organizations and Society* (June 1984): 383-406.

37. Ibid., 390-406.

38. W. G. Chase and H. A. Simon, "Perception in Chess," *Cognitive Psychology* 4 (1973): 55-87.

39. H. L. Chiesi, G. J. Spilich, and J. F. Voss, "Acquisition of Domain-Related Information in Relation to High and Low Domain Knowledge," *Journal of Verbal Learning and Verbal Behavior* 18 (1979): 257-73.

40. R. Halpern and H. G. Bower, "Musical Expertise and Melodic Structure in Memory for Musical Notation," *American Journal of Psychology* 95 (1982):31-50.

41. Schneiderman, "Exploratory Experiments in Programmer Behavior," *International Journal of Computer and Information Sciences* 5 (1976): 123-43.

42. McKeithen, et al., "Knowledge Organization and Skill Differences in Computer Programmers," 307-25.

43. B. Adelson, "Problem Solving and the Developing of Abstract Categories in Programming Languages," *Memory and Cognition* 9 (1981): 422-33.

44. B. Adelson, " When Novices Surpass Experts: The Difficulty of a Task May Increase with Expertise," *Journal of Experimental Psychology: Learning, Memory and Cognition* 10 (1984): 483-95.

45. R. Weber, "Some Characteristics of the Free Recall of Computer Controls by EDP Auditors," *Journal of Accounting Research* (Spring 1980): 214-41.

46. D. M. Frederick and R. Libby, "Expertise and Auditors' Judgments of Conjunctive Events," *Journal of Accounting Research* (Fall 1986): 770-90.

47. Michael Gibbins, "Proposition about the Psychology of Professional Judgment in Public Accounting," *Journal of Accounting Research* (Spring 1984): 103-25.

48. Michael Gibbins, "Knowledge Structures and Experienced Auditor Judgment," in Andrew Bailey, ed., *Auditor Productivity in the Year 2000: 1987 Proceedings of the Arthur Young Professors' Roundtable* (Reston, Va.: Arthur Young, 1988), 57.

49. Ibid., 51-73.

50. M. Gibbins, and C. Emby, "Evidence on the Nature of Professional Judgment in Public Accounting," in A. R. Abdel-Khalik and I. Solomon, eds., *Auditing Research Symposium* 1984 (Champaign, Ill.: University of Illinois at Urbana/Champaign, 1985), 181-212.

51. C. Emby and M. Gibbins, "Good Judgment in Public Accounting: Quality and Justification," *Contemporary Accounting Research* (Spring 1988): 287-313.

52. Similar models have been proposed for the performance appraisal process. See, e.g., A. S. De Nisi, T. P. Cafferty, and B. M. Meglino, "A Cognitive View of the Performance Appraisal Process: A Model and Research Proposition," *Organizational Behavior and Human Performance* 33 (1984): 360-96; J. M. Feldman, "Beyond Attribution Theory: Cognitive Processes in Performance Appraisal," *Journal of Applied Psychology* 66/2 (1981): 127-48.

53. H. H. Kelly, "Attributions in Social Interactions," in E. E. Jones et al., eds., *Attributions: Perceiving the Causes of Behavior* (Norristown, N. J.: General Learning Process, 1972).

54. B. Major, "Information Acquisition and Attribution Processes," *Journal of Personality and Social Psychology* 39 (1980): 1010-23.

55. De Nisi, Cafferty, and Meglino, " Performance Appraisal Decistion," 367-68.

56. Hl Tajfel, "Social Perception," in G. Lidzey and E. Aronson, eds., *Handbook of Social Psychology*, vol. 1 (Reading, Mass.: Addison-Wesley, 1969).

57. P. Slovic, B. Fischoff, and S. Lichtenstein, "Behavioral Decision Theory," *Annual Review of Psychology* 28 (1977): 119-39.

58. R. S. Wyer and T. K. Srull, "Category Accessibility: Some Theoretical and Empirical Issues Concerning the Processing of Social Stimulus Information," in E. Higgins, C. Herman, and M. Zarma, eds., *Social Cognition: The Ontario Symposium,* vol. 1 (Hillsdale, N.J.: Erlbaum, 1981).

59. M. Snyder and N. Cantor, "Treating Hypotheses about Other People: The Use of the Historical Knowledge," *Journal of Experimental Social Psychology* 15 (1979): 330-42.

60. M. Snyder, "Seek and Ye Shall Find: Testing Hypotheses about Other People," in M. Higgins, E. C. Herman, and M. Zarma, eds., *Social Cognition: The Ontario Symposium* (Hillsdale, N.J.: Erbaum, 1981), 1:33.

61. E. B. Ebbesen, "Cognitive Processes in Inferences about a Person's Personality," in M. Higgins, E. C. Herman, and M. Zarma, eds., *Social Cognition: The Ontario Symposium* (Hillsdale, N.J.: Erbaum, 1981), 1:55.

62. R. E. Nisbett and L. Ross, *Human Inference: Strategies and Shortcomings of Social Judgment* (Englewood Cliffs, N.J.: Trent and Hall, 1980), 7.

63. Wyer and Srull, "Category Accessibility."

64. Feldman, "Beyond Attribution Theory." 129.

65. M. Snyder and S. W. Uranowity, "Reconstructing the Past: Some Cognitive Consequences of Person Perception," *Journal of Personality and Social Psychology* 37 (1979): 1660-72.

66. E.Tulving, "Episodic and Semantic Memory," in E. Tulving and W. Donaldson, eds., *Organization of Memory* (New York: Academic Press, 1972).

67. R. C. Atkinson and R. M. Shiffrin, "Human Memory: A Proposed System and Its Control Processes," in K. W. Spence and J. T. Spence, eds., *Advances in the Psychology of Learning and Motivation Research and Theory,* vol. 2 (New York: Academic Press, 1968).

68. R. I. Craig, and R. S. Lockart, "Levels of Processing: A Framework for Memory Research," *Journal of Verbal Learning and Verbal Behavior* 11 (1972): 671-84.

69. R. Lachman, J. L. Lachman, and Earl C. Butterfield, *Cognitive Psychology and Information Processing: An Introduction* (Hillsdale, N.J.: Erlbaum, 1979), 274.

70. Walter Schneider and Richard M. Shiffrin, "Controlled and Automatic Human Information Processing: I. Detection, Search, and Attention," *Psychological Review* (Jan. 1977): 1-53.

71. Ibid., 51.

72. E. Tulving and Z. Pearlstone, "Availability versus Accessibility of Information in Memory for Words," *Journal of Verbal Learning and Verbal Behavior* 5 (1966): 381-91.

73. B. Hayes-Roth, "Evolution of Cognitive Structures and Processes," *Psychological Review* 84 (1977): 260-78.

74. P. W. Thorndyke and B. Hayes-Roth, “The Use of Shemata in the Acquisition and Transfer of Knowledge,” *Cognitive Psychology* 11 (1979): 86-87.

75. J. Perlmutter, P. Source, and J. L. Myers, “Retrieval Process in Recall,” *Cognitive Psychology* 8 (1976): 32-63.

76. B. Hayes-Roth and F. Hayes-Roth, “Plasticity in Memorial Networks,” *Journal of Verbal Learning and Verbal Behavior* (1979).

77. Ibid.

78. G. Greenwald, “Cognitive Learning, Cognitive Response to Pervasion(?), and Attitude Change,” in A. Greenwald, T. Brock, and T. Ostron, eds., *Psychological Foundations of Attitudes* (New York: Academic Press, 1960).

79. R. Schanke and R. Abelson, *Scripts, Plans, Goals, and Understanding* (Hillsdale, N.J.: Erlbaum, 1977).

80. T. K. Srull and R. S. Wyer, “Category Accessibility and Social Perception: Some Implications for the Study of Person, Memory and Interpersonal Judgments,” *Journal of Personality and Social Psychology* 38 (1980): 841-56.

81. K. P. Sentis and E. Burnstein, “Remembering Schema Consistent Information; Effects of Balance Schema on Recognition Memory,” *Journal of Personality and Social Psychology* 37 (1979): 2200-11.

82. C. E. Cohen, “Pearson Categories and Social Perception: Testing Some Boundaries of the Processing Effects of Prior Knowledge,” *Journal of Personality and Social Psychology* 40 (1981): 441-52.

83. S. E. Taylor, et al., “The Generalizability of Salience Effects,” *Journal of Personality and Social Psychology* 37 (1979): 357-68.

84. R. I. Craig and E. Tulving, "Depth of Processing and the Retention of Words in Episodic Memory," *Journal of Verbal Learning and Verbal Behavior* 11 (1972): 671-84.

85. R. Hastie and Bernadette Park, "The Relationship Between Memory and Judgment Depends on Whether the Judgment Task Is Memory-Based or On-Line," *Psychological Review* 93/3 (1986): 258-68.

86. E. J. Learner, A. Blank, and B. Chanowitz, "The Mindlessness of Ostensibly Thoughtful Action; The Role of Placebo Information in Interpersonal Interaction," *Journal of Personality and Social Psychology* 36 (1978): 635-42.

87. E. E. Learner, "False Models and Post-Data Model Construction," *Journal of the American Statistical Association* 69 (1974): 122-31.

88. E. E. Learner, "Explaining Your Results as Accent-Biased Memory," *Journal of the American Statistical Association* 70 (1975): 88-93.

89. M. Snyder and W. Uranowitz, "Reconstructing the Past: Some Cognitive Consequences of Person Perception," *Journal of Personality and Social Psychology* 36 (1978): 941-45.

90. C. Graesser and G. V. Nalsamura, "The Impact of Schema on Comprehension and Memory," *Psychology of Learning and Memory* 16 (1982): 60-102.

91. Graesser, Gordon, and Sawyer, "Memory for Typical and Atypical Actions in Scripted Activities," 319-32.

92. Chase and Simon, "Perception in Chess," 55-81.

93. G. Mandler, "From Association to Structure," *Psychological Review* 69 (1962): 415-27.

94. Ahmed Belkaoui, *Human Information Processing in Accounting* (Westport, Conn.: Quorum Books, 1989).

95. D. L. Hamilton and L. J. Huffman, "Generality of Impression Formation for Evaluative and Non-evaluative Judgments," *Journal of Personality and Social Psychology* 20 (1971): 200-207.

96. R. S. Wyer and H. L. Hinlete, "Information Factor Underlying Inferences about Hypothetical People," *Journal of Personality and Social Psychology* 34 (1976): 481-95.

97. Belkaoui, Human Information Processing in Accounting.

98. Ibid.

99. J. Jaynes, The Origin of Consciousness in the Breakdown of the Bicameral Mind (Toronto: University of Toronto Press, 1978).

100. R. E. Nisbett and T. D. Wilson, "Telling More Than We can Know: Verbal Reports on Mental Processes," *Psychological Review* (May 1977): 231-59.

101. Gibbins, "Propositions about the Psychology of Professional Judgment in Public Accounting," 113.

102. Belkaoui, Human Information Processing in Accounting.

103. R. M. Hogarth, Judgment and Choice: The Psychology of Decision (Chichester: Wiley, 1980).

104. Gibbins, "Propositions about the Psychology of Professional Judgment in Public Accounting," 114.

REFERENCES

Abelson, R. P. "The Psychological Status of the Script Concept." *American Psychologist* 36 (1981): 715-25.

Adelson, B. "When Novices Surpass Experts: The Difficulty of a Task May Increase with Expertise." *Journal of Experimental Psychology: Learning, Memory and Cognition* 10 (1984): 483-95.

———. "Problem Solving and the Development of Abstract Categories in Programming Languages." *Memory and Cognition* 9 (1981): 422-33.

Anderson, C. A. "Inoculation and Counter-Explanation: Debasing Techniques in the Perseverance of Social Theories." *Social Cognition* 1 (1982): 126-35.

Atkinson, R. C., and R. M. Shiffrin. "Human Memory: A Proposed System and Its Control Processes. In *Advances in the Psychology of Learning and Motivation Research and Theory,* edited by K.W. Spence and J. T. Spence, vol. 2. New York: Academic Press, 1968.

Bargh, J. A. "Attention and Automaticity in the Processing of Self-Relevant Information." *Journal of Personality and Social Psychology* 43 (1982): 425-36.

Bartlett, F. C. *Remembering.* London: Cambridge University Press, 1932.

Belkaoui, Ahmed. *Human Information Processing in Accounting.* Westport, Conn.: Quorum Books, 1989.

Bobrow, D. G., and D. A. Norman. "Some Principles of Memory Schemata." In *Representations and Understanding: Studies in Cognitive Science,* edited by D. G. Bobrow and A. M. Collins. New York: Academic Press, 1975.

Brewer, W. F., and G. V. Nalsamura. "The Nature and Functions of Schemas." In R. S. Wyer, Jr., and T. K. Scrull, *Handbook of Social Cognition* (Hillsdale, N.J.: Erlbaum, 1984), 139-50.

Canton, N., and W. Mischel. "Prototypes in Person Perception." In *Advances in Experimental Psychology,* edited by L. Berkowitz, vol. 12. New York: Academic Press, 1979.

Chase, W. G., and H. A. Simon, "The Mind's Eye in Chess." In *Visual Information Processing,* edited by W. G. Chase. New York: Academic Press, 1983.

———. "Perception in Chess." *Cognitive Psychology* 4 (1973): 55-87.

Chi, M. T. H., and R. Koeske, "Network Representations of a Child's Dinosaur Knowledge." *Developmental Psychology* 19 (1983): 29-35.

Chiesi, H. L., G. J. Spilich, and J. F. Voss, "Acquisition of Domain-Related Information in Relation to High and Low Domain Knowledge." *Journal of Verbal Learning and Verbal Behavior* 18 (1979): 257-73.

Cohen, C. E. "Pearson Categories and Social Perception: Testing Some Boundaries of the Processing Effects of Prior Knowledge." *Journal of Personality and Social Psychology* 40 (1981): 441-52.

Craig, R. I., and R. S. Lochart, “Levels of Processing: A Framework for Memory Research,” *Journal of Verbal Learning and Verbal Behavior* 11 (1972): 671-84.

Craig, R. I., and E. Tulving, “Depth of Processing and the Retention of Words in Episodic Memory.” *Journal of Verbal Learning and Verbal Behavior* 11 (1972): 671-84.

De Nisi, A. S., T. P. Cafferty, and B. M. Meglino. “A Cognitive View of the Performance Appraisal Process: A Model and Research Proposition.” *Organizational Behavior and Human Performance* 33 (1984): 360-96.

Ebbesen, E. B. “Cognitive Processes in Inferences about a Person’s Personality.” In M. Higgins, E. C. Herman, and M. Zarma, *Social Cognition: The Ontario Symposium* (Hillsdale, N.J.: Erlbaum, 1984), 52-59.

Emby, C. and M. Gibbins. “Good Judgment in Public Accounting: Quality and Justification.” *Contemporary Accounting Research* (Spring 1988): 287-313.

Feldman, Jack M. “Beyond Attribution Theory: Cognitive Processes in Performance Appraisal.” *Journal of Applied Psychology* 66/2 (1981): 127-48.

Felix, W. L., Jr., and W. R. Kinney, Jr. “Research in the Auditor’s Opinion Formulation Process: State of the Art.” *Accounting Review* (Apr. 1988): 245-71.

Ferguson, T. J., B. G. Rule, and D. Carlson. “Memory for Personally Relevant Information.” *Journal of Personality and Social Psychology* 44 (1983): 251-61.

Fiske, S. T., and S. E. Taylor, *Social Cognition* (New York: Random House, 1984), 154.

Fredeirick, D. M., and R. Libby. "Expertise and Auditors' Judgments of Conjunctive Events." *Journal of Accounting Research* (Fall 1986), 220-90.

Gibbins, Michael. "Knowledge Structures and Experienced Auditor Judgment." In *Auditor Productivity in the Year 2000: 1987 Proceedings of the Arthur Young Professors' Roundtable,* edited by Andrw Bailey, p. 57. Reston, Va.: Arthur Young, 1988.

———. "Proposition about the Psychology of Professional Judgment in Public Accounting." *Journal of Accounting Research* (Spring 1984): 103-25.

Gibbins, M., and C. Emby. "Evidence on the Nature of Professional Judgment in Public Accounting." In *Auditing Research Symposium 1984* edited by A. R. Abdel-Khalik and I. Solomon, pp. 181-212. Champaign, Ill.: University of Illinois at Urbana/Champaign, 1985.

Graesser, A. C., S. E. Gordon, and J. D. Sawyer. "Memory for Typical and Atypical Actions in Scripted Activities: Test of a Script Pointer + Tag Hypothesis." *Journal of Verbal Learning and Behavior* 18 (1979): 319-32, 503-15.

Graesser, A. C., and G. V. Nalsamura. "The Impact of Schema on Comprehension and Memory." *Psychology of Learning and Memory* 16 (1982): 60-102.

Greenwald, A. G. "Cognitive Learning, Cognitive Response to Pervasion(?), and Attitude Change." In *Psychological*

Foundations of Attitudes, edited by A. Greenwald, T. Brock, and T. Ostron. New York: Academic Press, 1960.

Halpern, A. R., and H. G. Bower. "Musical Expertise and Melodic Structure in Memory for Musical Notation." *American Journal of Psychology* 95 (1982): 31-50.

Hamilton, D. L., and L. J. Huffman. "Generality of Impression Formation for Evaluative and Non-evaluative Judgments." *Journal of Personality and Social Psychology* 20 (1971): 200-207.

Hastie, R. "Memory for Behavioral Information That Confirms or Contradicts a Personality Impression." In *Person Memory: The Cognitive Basis of Social Perception,* edited by R. Hastie, et al. Hillsdale, N.J.: Erlbaum, 1981.

Hastie, R., and Bernadette Park. "The Relationship Between Memory and Judgment Depends on Whether the Judgment Task Is Memory-Based or On-Line." *Psychological Review* 93/3 (1986): 258-68.

Hayes-Roth, B., and F. Hayes-Roth. "Plasticity in Memorial Networks." *Journal of Verbal Learning and Verbal Behavior* (1979).

Hogarth, R. M. Judgment and Choice: The Psychology of Decision. Chichester: Wiley, 1980.

Jaynes, J. The Origin of Consciousness in the Breakdown of the Bicameral Mind. Toronto: University of Toronto Press, 1978.

Kelly, H. H. "Attributions in Social Interactions." In *Attributions: Perceiving the Causes of Behavior,* edited by E. E. Jones. Norristown, N.J.: General Learning Process, 1972.

Kuiper, N. A. "Convergent Evidence for the Self as a Prototype." *Personality and Social Psychology Bulletin* 7 (1981): 438-43.

Lachman, R., J. L. Lachman, and Earl C. Butterfield. *Cognitive Psychology and Information Processing: An Introduction.* Hillsdale, N.J.: Erlbaum, 1979.

Larkin, J. H., et al. "Models of Competence in Solving Physics Problems." *Science* 200 (1980): 1335-42.

Learner, E. E. "Explaining Your Results as Accent-Biased Memory." *Journal of the American Statistical Association* 70 (1975): 88-93.

———. "False Models and Post-Data Model Construction." *Journal of the American Statistical Association* 69 (1974): 122-31.

Learner, E. J., A. Blank, and B. Chanowitz. "The Mindlessness of Ostensibly Thoughtful Action: The Role of Placebo Information in Interpersonal Interaction." *Journal of Personality and Social Psychology* 36 (1978): 635-42.

Linville, P. W., and E. E. Jones. "Polonized Appraisals of Outgroup Members." *Journal of Personality and Social Psychology* 42 (1982): 193-211.

McKeithen, K. B., et al. "Knowledge Organization and Skill Differences in Computer Programmers." *Cognitive Psycholgoy* 13 (1981): 307-25.

Major, B. "Information Acquisition and Attribution Processes." *Journal of Personality and Social Psychology* 39 (1980): 1010-23.

Malpass, R. S., H. Lavingnern, and D. E. Weldon. "Verbal and Visual Training in Face Recognition." *Perception and Psychophysics* 14 (1973): 285-92.

Mandler, G. "From Association to Structure." *Psychological Review* 69 (1962): 415-27.

Mandler, Jean. "Categorical and Schematic Organization in Memory." In *Memory, Organization and Structure,* edited by R. C. Ruff. New York: Academic Press, 1979.

Markus, H. "Self-Schemata and Processing Information about the Self." *Journal of Personality and Social Psychology* 38 (1980): 231-48.

Markus, H., and K. P. Sentis. "The Self in Social Information Processing." In *Psychological Perspectives on the Self,* edited by J. Suls. Vol. 1. Hillsdale, N.J.: Erlbaum, 1982.

Nisbett, R. E., and L. Ross. *Human Inference: Strategies and Shortcomings of Social Judgment.* Englewood Cliffs, N.J.: Trent and Hall, 1980.

Nisbett, R.E., and T. D. Wilson. "Telling More Than We Can Know: Verbal Reports on Mental Processes." *Psychological Review* (May 1977): 231-59.

Perlmutter, J., P. Source, and J. L. Myers. "Retrieval Process in Recall." *Cognitive Psychology* 8 (1976): 32-63.

Rankus, H. "Self-Schema DNA Processing Information about the Self." *Journal of Personality and Social Psychology* 35 (1977): 63-78.

Ross, L., M. R. Lepper, and M. Hubard. "Perseverance in Self-Perception and Social Perception: Biased Attribution Processes in the Debriefing Paradigm." *Journal of Personality and Social Psychology* 32 (1975): 880-92.

Rumelhart, D. E. "Schemata and the Cognitive System." In *Handbook of Social Cognition*, edited by R. S. Wyer, Jr., and T.K. Srull. Vol. 1. Hillsdale, N.J.: Erlbaum, 1984.

Schanke, R., and R. Abelson. *Scripts, Plans, Goals, and Understanding*. Hillsdale, N.J.: Erlbaum, 1977.

Schneider, Walter, and Richard M. Shriffrin. "Controlled and Automatic Human Information Processing: I. Detection, Search, and Attention." *Psychological Review* (Jan. 1977): 1-53.

Schneiderman, B. "Exploratory Experiments in Programmer Behavior." *International Journal of Computer and Information Sciences* 5 (1976): 123-43.

Sentis, K. P., and E. Burnstein. "Remembering Schema Consistent Information: Effects of Balance Schema on Recognition Memory." *Journal of Personality and Social Psychology* 37 (1979): 2200-11.

Slovic, P., B. Fischoff, and S. Lichtenstein. "Behavioral Decision Theory." *Annual Review of Psychology* 28 (1977): 119-39.

Snyder, N., and N. Cantor. "Treating Hypotheses about Other People: The Use of the Historical Knowledge." *Journal of Experimental Social Psychology* 15 (1979): 330-42.

Snyder, M., and S. W. Uranowity. "Reconstructing the Past: Some Cognitive Consequences of Person Perception." *Journal of Personality and Social Psychology* 37 (1979): 941-45, 1660-72.

Srull, T. K., and R. S. Wyer. "Category Accessibility and Social Perception: Some Implications for the Study of Person, Memory and Interpersonal Judgments." *Journal of Personality and Social Psychology,* 38 (1980): 841-56.

Tajfel, Hl. "Social Perception." In *Handbook of Social Psychology,* edited by G. Lidzey and E. Aronson. Vol. 1. Reading, Mass.: Addison-Wesley, 1969.

Taylor, S. E., and J. Crocker. "Schematic Bases of Social Information Processing." In *Social Cognition: The Ontario Symposium,* edited by E. t. Higgins, C. P. Herman, and M. P. Zanna. Vol. 1. Hillsdale, N.J.: Erlbaum, 1981.

Taylor, S. E., J. Aoker, S. T. Fiske, M. Springer, and J. Winkler. "The Generalizability of Salience Effects." *Journal of Personality and Social Psychology* 37 (1979): 357-68.

Taylor, S. E., S. T. Fiske, N. L. Etcoff, and A. J. Ruderman. "Categorical Bases of Person Memory and Stereotyping." *Journal of Personality and Social Psychology* 36 (1978): 778-93.

Thorndyke, P. W., and B. Hayes-Roth. "The Use of Schemata in the Acquisition and Transfer of Knowledge." *Cognitive Psychology* 11 (1979): 86-87.

Tulving, E. "Episodic and Semantic Memory." In *Organizatino of Memory*, editecd by E. Tulving and W. Donaldson. New York: Academic Press, 1972.

Tulving, E., and Z. Pearlstone. "Availability versus Accessibility of Information in Memory for Words." *Journal of Verbal Learning and Verbal Behavior* 5 (1966): 381-91.

Waller, W. S., and W. L. Felix, Jr. "The Auditor and Learning from Experience: Some conjectures." *Accounting, Organizations and Society* (June 1984): 383-406.

Weber, R. "Some Characteristics of the Free Recall of Computer Controls by EDP Auditors." *Journal of Accounting Research* (Spring 1980): 214-41.

Woodswork, R. S., and H. Schlosberg. *Experimental Psychology.* New York: Holt, 1954.

Wyer, R. S. Jr., and S. E. Gordon. "The Cognitive Representation of Social Information." In *Handbook of Social Cognition*, edited by R. S. Wyer, Jr., and T. K. Srull. Vol. 2 Hillsdale, N.J.: Erlbaum, 1984.

Wyer, R. S., and H. L. Hinlele. "Informational Factor Underlying Inferences about Hypothetical People." *Journal of Personality and Social Psychology* 34 (1976): 481-95.

Wyer, R. S. and T. K. Srull. "Category Accessibility: Some Theoretical and Empirical Issues Concerning the Processing of Social Stimulus Information." In *Social Cognition: The Ontario Symposium,* edited by E. Higgins, C. Herman, and M. Zanna. Vol. 1. Hillsdale, N.J.: Erlbaum, 1981.

5. FUNCTIONAL AND DATA FIXATION

INTRODUCTION

Functional fixation, as it is used in information management, suggests that under certain circumstances a decision maker might be unable to adjust his or her decision process to a change in the information process that supplied him or her with input data. Borrowed from the literature of psychology, the phenomenon has been used in a slightly different way by researchers in information management. The purposes of this chapter are, first, to differentiate between the functional-fixation phenomenon as it is understood in psychology and the data-fixation phenomenon as it is used in information management; second, to examine the results of the various experimental studies in the area; and third, to provide possible theoretical explanations of the phenomenon and to suggest better methodologies for studying the phenomenon in information management.

NATURE OF FUNCTIONAL FIXATION

Functional Fixation in Psychology

Functional fixation originated as a concept in psychology, arising from an investigation of the impact of past experience on human behavior. In his examination of the relation between stimulus equivalence and reasoning, Maier identified several ways in which past experience can affect the problem-solving process.[1] He viewed past experience as a salient factor in problem solving, in that problem solving can be facilitated by equivalences that exist in immediate problem situations and in past experiences. In addition, the background of past learning is an essential repertoire of behavior that is available for restructuring when it is needed for new situations. Not all psychologists, however, have viewed past experience as a positive factor. Some have seen it as an obstacle that prevents productive thinking. Duncker introduced the concept of functional fixation to illustrate the negative role of past experiences.[2] He investigated the hypothesis that an individual's prior use of an object in a function dissimilar to that required in a present problem would serve to inhibit the discovery of an appropriate, novel use for the object. His results supported the functional-fixation hypothesis with regard to several common objects, for example, boxes, pliers, weights, and paper clips. Birch and Rabinowitz criticized Duncker's experiments, showing that an individual can also learn about an object's versatility and therefore display a relatively low degree of fixation even if learning about one function of an object restricts the number of ways in which it is used.[3] A series of experiments by Flavell, Cooper, and Loisell supported this conclusion.[4]

Others who have refined Duncker's experiments nevertheless have supported the functional-fixation hypothesis. Adamson, in his box experiment, gave subjects the task of attaching three small candles to a screen, at a height of about five feet, using to accomplish the task any of a large number of objects that were lying on the table, namely three pasteboard boxes, five matches, and five thumbtacks.[5] The solution consisted of putting one candle on each box by melting wax on the box, sticking the candle to the box, and then tacking the boxes to the screen. The idea was to have the box be used as platform on which to attach the candle, a novel function for boxes. Two groups were used. The experimental one was presented with the objects inside the box; the control group had the objects on the table. "Hence, the boxes had their initial function, that of containing, whereas in their solution function, they had to be used as supports or platforms."[6] The results showed that the control group outperformed the experimental group in terms of both the number of solutions and the time required to reach the solutions. This suggested that the subjects in the experimental group were functionally fixated on using boxes as containers rather than as platforms.

In the two-string experiments, Adamson and Taylor asked their subjects to tie together the free ends of strings hanging from the ceiling.[7] Because the strings were placed so far apart, the problem could be solved only by trying a weight to one string, swinging it like a pendulum, and catching it while holding the other string. The task then could be completed by tying the two strings together. Of the various objects provided to the subjects, only two—an electrical switch and an electrical relay—were sufficiently heavy to serve as weights. Half of the subjects were trained before the experiment to use the switch to complete an electrical circuit, while the other half were trained to use a relay for the same task. The results of the experiment supported that functional-fixation hypothesis for the reason that the subjects trained to use the switch to complete the circuit used the relay to solve the two-string task, while those who had been trained to use the relay to complete the circuit used the switch as a pendulum weight. This fixation phenomenon was reported in a series of other experiments.[8] The degree of fixity also was found to depend on some mediating factors, such as the span of time since the object was previously used,[9] the necessity of using the object in a novel way to solve the problem,[10] hints,[11] and intelligence.[12]

Data Fixation in Information Management

Ijiri, Jaedicke, and Knight viewed the decision process as being characterized by three factors: decision inputs, decision outputs, and decision rules. They then introduced the conditions under which a decision maker cannot adjust his or her decision process to a change in the information process. For example, changes in depreciation methods or inventory techniques lead to different profit figures. Ijiri, Jaedicke, and Knight attributed the inability to adjust, if it existed, to the psychological factor of functional fixation.[13] They stated:

> Psychologists have found that there appears to be functional fixation in most human behavior in which the person attaches a meaning to a title or object (e.g., manufacturing cost) and is unable to see alternative meanings or uses. People intuitively associate a value

> with an item through past experience, and often do not recognize that the value of the item depends, in fact, upon the particular moment in time and may be significantly different from what it was in the past. Therefore, when a person is placed in a new situation, he views the object or term as used previously.[14]

To link the psychological concept of functional fixation to information management, they merely stated the following:

> If the outputs from different accounting methods are called by the same name, such as profit, costs, etc., people who do understand accounting well tend to neglect the fact that alternative methods may have been used to prepare the outputs. In such cases, a change in the accounting process clearly influences the decisions.[15]

This extrapolation of a psychological concept to information management is welcome if it is interpreted correctly. The literature now recognizes the point that the focus in psychology is on functions, whereas Ijiri, Jaedicke, and Knight focused on outputs. If we go back to the example of a change in inventory techniques, functional fixation in psychology implies that the decision makers are accustomed to using the data for one function (such as price decisions) and now fail to see its potential use for another function (for example, production decisions). As introduced by

Ijiri, Jaedicke, and Knight, functional fixation implies that decision makers are fixated on the information output (for example, the profit output) and are unable to adjust to see that the change in output is due to the change in inventory techniques. Thus, while psychologists are interested in functional fixation involving functions or objects, accounting research, influenced by Ijiri, Jaedicke, and Knight's extrapolation, is interested in functional fixation involving data. One might assume correctly that most of the interest in psychology has been on functional fixation. The exceptions to this assumption are a psychological data-fixation study by Knight and a mixed data-fixation/functional-fixation study in accounting by Barnes and Webb.[16] Ashton also has recognized the difference between the two views of functional fixation in information management and psychology.[17] He came to a peculiar conclusion, however, when he stated:

> We should recognize that the functional fixation hypothesis in accounting is a modified form (or forms) of the hypothesis in psychology. The modified functional hypothesis should be subjected to research in accounting contexts, rather than relying entirely on the original functional fixation research as Ijiri, Jaedicke, Knight, and subsequent researchers appear to have done.[18]

-The approach should consider two forms of the functional-fixation hypothesis, one focusing on function and one focusing on output or data. There lies the main difference: in the case of functional fixation, psychologists used objects such as medallions, string, and boxes to solve relatively simple tasks, whereas the data-fixation experiments all used data to solve unstructured problems.

DATA-FIXATION RESEARCH IN INFORMATION MANAGEMENT

DATA-FIXATION RESEARCH BASED ON THE IJIRI-JAEDICKE-KNIGHT PARADIGM

Functional-fixation research in information management generally has followed Ijiri, Jaedicke, and Knight's prescriptions, focusing on data rather than function, and has led to a series of data-fixation experiments. Ashton used M.B.A. students to assess the extent to which individual decision makers alter their decision processes after occurrence of an accounting change, from full-cost to variable-cost data, as evidenced by the effect of this cognitive change on subsequent decisions.[19] Ashton not only discussed the accounting change with the subjects but also mentioned whether it reflected more or less important informational content, and consequently may have dictated a change in the decision behavior of the subjects. This result suggests that a large proportion of subjects in the experimental groups failed to adjust significantly their decision process in response to the information change, thereby providing evidence of the existence of functional fixation in information management. The study was not met with complete approval. First, Libby criticized it for an experimental design that might have become confounded with the effects of the information change.[20] He concluded that

> Serious questions concerning the way in which the conceptual network was operationalized, coupled with methodology deficiencies, question whether any conclusions can change the subjects, the manipulation of the moderating variables information and importance, and the method of measuring the change in the subject's decision process.[21]

Second, Pearson, a practitioner, simply rejected the study's objectives and results as irrelevant to information management.[22] These criticisms, as might be expected, motivated further empirical research.

Swieringa, Dyckman, and Hoskin looked into Libby's criticisms and found that subjects tended to adjust their information processing as a result of the information change even though the significance of these adjustments differed depending on how they were measured.[23] The amount of information provided was found to influence the subjects' adjustments of their information processing. Swieringa, Dyckman, and Hoskin had made two modifications in Ashton's experimental design. One modification was to isolate the effects of the amount and form of the information about the information change. The second modification was to have the data received by the control groups be equivalent to the data received by the experimental groups.

A second study by Dyckman, Hoskin, and Swieringa merely replicated the earlier study by Swieringa, Dyckman, and Hoskin with subjects who, on average, were older and had more exposure to accounting and business matters.[24] The students used in the first study were enrolled in an introductory accounting course in a college of agriculture and life sciences and did not know what direct costing meant. In addition, the second study relied on a cross-sectional approach instead of a time-series approach to analyze the effects of the experimental conditions and demographic variables on the prices set by the subjects for each product. The results of the second study were found to be similar to those of the first one.

In their experiment, Chang and Birnberg provided M.B.A. students with a cost variance report and a cost standard.[25] The subjects were required to indicate (1) whether they would investigate the production process, and (2) how large a variance would be necessary to justify an investigation. Their results pointed to the existence of a "weak form" of data fixity when a change in the variance amount was introduced. The "weak form" label was used to characterize a slight change in behavior; no change in behavior was evidence of the "strong form" of fixity. Two significant finds were noted by the authors:

> First, fixity is not a phenomenon that is unavoidable. Research indicates that once we are aware of its presence, we can take steps to cope with it. The real question becomes one of finding the manner in which it can be reduced and efficient ways of doing so. Second, unfortunately, once alerted to the problem, there is reason to believe that the subject's behavior will continue to reflect elements of past behavior—behavior which should have been forgotten along with the superseded data set. This then suggests two topics

> for future research. One is how past experience affects the subject's behavior. The other is how to extinguish the older, now unnecessary patterns of behavior.[26]

Abdel-Khalik and Keller used bank investment offices and security analysts in their investigation of functional fixation.[27] They articulated their research problems as follows:

> If investors are functionally fixated on the use of reported accounting earnings, then they will tend to ignore other accounting information which is not consistent with accounting numbers. The accounting signal which we chose to be inconsistent with reported earnings is the decision of management to switch the method of inventory valuation from First-in, First-out (FIFO) or from average cost to Last-in, First-out (LIFO) for both accounting and tax purposes.[28]

Because of the higher cash flows that result from change to LIFO in a period of rising prices, the investor using a cash-flow discounted model would value the firm higher, while another relying and fixated on earnings would value it lower. The results of the experiment showed evidence of functional fixation, as the subjects relied on the adjusted net income rather than cash flows in evaluating the securities. One problem with Abdel-Khalik and Keller's study is the fact that the firms that switched to LIFO received qualified audit opinions, while those on FIFO obtained unqualified opinions. This could explain why the LIFO firms generally were viewed as having lower expected returns.

Bloom, Elgers, and Murray extended the Ashton study by examining both individual and group decisions in response to a fully disclosed, cosmetic change in depreciation method.[29] The results of the study showed a moderate shift in the decision behavior of individuals, a phenomenon similar to what Chang and Birnberg called the weak form of fixation. In addition, they found that groups exhibited a higher degree of fixation than did individuals. Among the reasons given for this difference were the following: "One explanation is that the group process inhibited the collective or individual intellectual functioning of its members; yet another is that the groups incurred a higher cost in developing a new decision rule in response to the accounting change than did the individuals."[30]

Another explanation was that the difference could be a reflection of the nature of the task, which consisted of the need both to reach a decision within the group on a decision rule and to make a decision on the task.[31]

Another information management study provided evidence of functional fixation without being based on Ashton's and Ijiri, Jaedicke, and Knight's paradigms. A National Association of Accountants (NAA) research study on the effects of software accounting policies on bank lending decisions and stock prices showed clear evidence of fixation by loan officers making a decision on a loan to two fictional firms: the Campbell Corporation, which capitalized software expenditures; and the Edwards Corporation, which expensed all software costs.[32] Without mentioning data fixation per se, the results were indicative of the presence of the phenomenon. Witness the following:

> Campbell was favored over Edwards by 62.2% of the respondents; Edwards was favored by 11.1%; 13.3% would treat the companies equally, but did not give any reason for the equal treatment; and 13.3% would treat the companies equally because a company's software policy would not influence the lending decision. Only 27.3% of the bankers would grant a $3 million, five year unsecured loan to Edwards; compare with 61.4% for Campbell. Of those respondents that gave an interest rate for both companies, 55% would charge Campbell a lower rate, 5% would charge Edwards a lower rate, and 40% would charge the same rate to both companies.[33]

A similar finding was made in another study. Belkaoui conducted an experiment in which bank loan officers evaluated a loan application that was accompanied by financial statements based on either accrual or modified cash accounting.[34] The loan officers in the experiment believed that the loan applicant presenting accrual accounting financial statements (1) was more likely to repay the loan, (2) was more likely to be granted the loan, (3) was given a different interest rate premium, and (4) had statements that were more reliable and freer of clerical errors.

Other Data-Fixation Research

Other information management research studies have used the Ijiri-Jaedicke-Knight paradigm to explain their own results. This strategy has taken place both in the research of investor decisions and in capital market research.

In the research of investor decisions, a cross-sectional orientation was given to functional fixation as it was applied to alternative accounting methods rather than to changes in accounting methods over time. Jensen examined the impact of alternative depreciation and inventory costing methods on investor decisions.[35] To explain his findings that alternative accounting techniques affected decision making, he suggested that his subjects might be functionally fixated on net earnings. Livingstone examined the effects of alternative, interperiod tax-allocation methods on regulatory rate-of-return decisions affecting the electric utility industry.[36] In light of his finds that some rate-making books focus on "raw" rates of return and ignore the effects of alternative tax-allocation methods, he offered the explanation that some predictions might be functionally fixated on net operating revenue. Livingstone stated the following:

It is therefore hypothesized that the reason that original-cost jurisdictions have been so much slower to adjust for alternative treatments of deferred taxes is that they are functionally fixated with respect to financial statement data. Since normalizing changes the amount but not the name of net operating revenue, it is intended that original-cost juries-dictions tend to view net operating revenue under normalizing as being the same as without it.[37]

Livingstone also suggested that users of accounting information could have formed a learning set after having experience with a significant number of different problems, all of which can be solved in the same manner. One solution went as follows: "If the hypothesis of a learning set with respect to alternative accounting methods is valid, multi-informational accounting statements would tend to stimulate learning and reduce functional fixation by providing users with information on accounting alternatives."[38] Mlynarezyk examined the effect of alternative tax-accounting methods on common-stock prices of electric utility companies and related functional fixation to his work.[39]

In capital market research, the functional-fixation hypothesis has been used to explain the lack of efficiency in the capital market. Beaver argued, however, that the market is not functionally fixated.[40] He stated the following:

In essence, the implication of the functional fixation hypothesis is that two firms (securities) could be alike in all "real" economic respects and yet sell for different prices, simply because of the way the accountant reported the results of operations. The implication is that the market ignores the fact that observed signals are generated from different information systems. Hence, it does not distinguish between numbers generated by different accounting methods either over time or across firms. Needless to say, this implies market inefficiency.... The functional fixation hypothesis as described above is a rather extreme form of the market inefficiency argument, in that it implies that disequilibrium could exist indefinitely and presumably permanently.[41]

DATA FIXATION AND FUNCTIONAL FIXATION IN ACCOUNTING AND PSYCHOLOGY

As stated earlier, most information management research has focused on data fixation, while psychological research has focused on functional fixation. The exceptions to this are a data-fixation study in psychology by Knight and a mixed data-fixation functional-fixation study in accounting by Barnes and Webb.[42]

Knight *conducted* an experiment to investigate the impact of the successful solving of *n* water jug problems on the problem-solving techniques used in trial *n+1*. The results showed that a series of successes caused the subject to persist in his early behavior, making it difficult for him to see the alternative (correct) approach. Furthermore, the subject would give complex, correct solutions to even trivial problems in cases where the complex solutions had led to successful results in the previous *n* trials.

Barnes and Webb were interested in the investigation of both the data-fixation and the functional-fixation hypothesis in accounting. Actual managers were asked to make price decisions based on real-life case studies that differed in their method of inventory valuation (full costing versus direct costing). The data-fixation hypothesis was confirmed in that the subjects were fixated by the total costs figure, altering their projected price in response to the changes in reported costs caused by the measurement change. However, the functional-fixation hypothesis was not confirmed because the subjects did not try to recover overhead costs, even though they were instructed that this was necessary, simply because they were not used to doing so. The lack of evidence for the functional-fixity hypothesis, a phenomenon widely observed in psychology, was attributed to the use of highly experienced and intelligent scientists. This is not surprising since intelligence has been found to mitigate fixity.[43]

DETERMINANTS OF FUNCTIONAL FIXATION IN INFORMATION MANAGEMENT

The Conditioning Hypothesis

The impact of information data on users and their behavior has always been a subject of interest for social scientists. One extreme concern, expressed by Schumpeter, goes as follows:

> Capitalist practice turns the unit of money into a tool of rational cost-profit calculations, of which the towering monument is double-entry bookkeeping.... Primarily a product of the evolution of economic rationality, the cost-profit calculus in turn reacts upon that rationality; by crystallizing and defining numerically, it powerfully peoples the logic of enterprise....This type of logic or attribute or method then starts upon its conqueror's career subjugating—rationalizing—man's tools and philosophies, his medical practice, his picture of the cosmos, his outlook on life, everything in fact including his concepts of beauty and justice and his spiritual ambitions.[44]

Information management researchers have not reached the point of Schumpeter's consensus, but they also have stressed the notion that the socialization of accountants, with its emphasis on particular cost and income considerations, can lead to a form of conditioning and might explain some of the empirically observed decision processes. The argument is that users, individually or in aggregate, react because they have been conditioned to react to accounting data rather than because the data have any informational content. For example, Sterling contends that

> if the response of receivers to accounting stimuli is to be taken as evidence that certain kinds of accounting practices are justified, then we must not overlook the possibility that those responses were conditioned. Accounting reports have been issued for a long time, and their issuance has been accompanied by a rather impressive ceremony performed by the managers and accountants who issue them. The receivers are likely to have gained the impression that they ought to react and have noted that others react, and thereby have become conditioned to react.[45]

It may also be argued that the recipients of accounting information react when they should not react or should not react the way they do. The conditioning hypothesis has also been advanced by Revsine as follows:

> The process by which users may be conditioned to the data they receive could occur in at least two ways. First, as students in business training curricula, the prospective students are introduced to generally accepted accounting principles and the financial

statements that result from the applications of these principles and their derivative procedures. Furthermore, they are taught manipulative operations and techniques such as ratio and funds flow analysis that utilize accounting data as a means of evaluating enterprise performance and prospects. In short, users are generally indoctrinated concerning the relevance and utility of traditionally disseminated information. Second, this formal conditioning is continually reinforced by each external report that users receive.[46]

One explanation of the data-fixation findings may be that subjects of the experiments, mostly accounting students, have been conditioned to react to some form of accounting outputs (for instance, cost or income income outputs), and have failed to adjust their decision processes in response to a "well-disclosed" accounting change. The conditioning phenomenon inhibits the subjects from adopting the correct behavior, which is to adjust to the accounting change, and has led them to act as they have been conditioned to act in their previous behaviors or socialization sessions. Thus, the phenomenon is a form of functional fixation, as the subjects no longer are able to discriminate.

Prospect Theory and the Framing Hypothesis

Kahneman and Tversky's prospect theory states that potential gains and losses are evaluated by an S-shaped value, function, one that is convex (indicating a risk-averse orientation) for losses.[47] Four effects are observable in the process of choosing among bets:

Certainty effect: "People overweigh outcomes that are considered certain relative to outcomes which are merely probable."[48]

Reflection effect: "The selection of prospects around 0 reverses the preference orders."[49]

Aversion to probabilistic insurance: Subjects do not like the idea of probabilistic insurance because it pays off with a probability of less-than-one but diminishes the premium.

Isolation effect: "In order to simplify the choice between alternatives, people often disregard components that distinguish them."[50]

The concept of framing options adds the key idea that the frame of the decision is simply the decision maker's concept of the decision problem or its structure. The frame is defined as follows: "The decision-maker's conception of the acts, outcomes and contingencies [is] associated with a particular choice. The frame that a decision-maker adopts is controlled partly by the formulation of the problem and partly by the norms, habits and personal characteristics of the decision-maker."[51]

Framing occurs because the wording of a question has the potential to alter a subject's response. Functional fixation may be viewed as a result of the particular choice of framing options made by the subjects in the experiments. The formulation of the decision tasks as well as the norms, habits, and personal characteristics of the subjects affect the framing of the decision and lead to the functional- or data-fixation results.

Interference Theory: Stimulus Encoding versus Retroactive Intuition

The learning theory holds that prior knowledge can either interfere with or facilitate effective decision making. The interference theory emerged from the two possible outcomes of the transfer-of-training hypothesis. According to the latter hypothesis, the transfer of training may have either facilitating or inhibitory effects. When a subject learns two tasks, task 1 and task 2, then is asked to perform task 1. the effects of the transfer of training are as follows: "Transfer may facilitate the learning of the second task, or conceivably have an inhibitory effect and interfere with the second learning and the mastery of the second task may help or hinder the subsequent performance of the first task"[52] What results, then, are two possible effects:

A negative transfer is labeled retroactive inhibition or retroactive interference.[53] In such a case the learning of task 2 affects the performance of the first task. The design used for the study of retroactive interference is as follows:[54]

Experimental group: Learn Task Learn Task 2 Test Task 1

Control group: Learn Task 1 Test Task 1

Functional fixity has been viewed as "a classic case of negative transfer."

A positive or facilitator effect is labeled *retroactive facilitation*. This positive transfer motivates the stimulus-encoding hypothesis, whereby a distinction is made between the nominal stimulus provided by the experiments and the functional stimulus perceived by the subject. No functional fixity would result from the stimulus-encoding process.[55]

Haka, Friedman, and Jones used the above interference theory to test the hypothesis that exposure to cost and income measures causes fixated responses in a decision-making setting where market value is the appropriate response."[56] If subjects are presented with two stimulus-response pairs for market price (*A-B*) and one for cost or income (*C-D*), with separate stimulus and responses for each, and if C is confused with *A*, resulting in an *A-B, C-B* paradigm, then response *B* becomes the fixated response because of retroactive interference. In other words:

The hypothesis posited that prevalence of cost and profit information interferes with (that is, causes fixation) or facilitates appropriate market-based decision models. In particular, if stimulus encoding is dominant, then subjects with more cost and profit exposure should be more likely to use the market price data than those with less exposure. If retroactive inhibition dominates, then the opposite effect should be discerned.[57]

The results of the study did not support the proposition that exposure to accounting concepts in accounting courses interferes with decision processes. In addition, only some moderate support was found for the theory that stimulus encoding causes some retroactive facilitation.

Primacy versus Recency and Ego Involvement

The findings on data fixation in information management for the most part have been obtained by having students placed in a stressful situation make a given choice (for example, a price decision) before and after an accounting change. The students know the nature of the accounting change (such as from full costing to variable costing) from their courses and the learning process preceding the experiment. A relevant research question would be the impact of this learning order on the acceptance of accounting techniques and on the results observed in data-fixation research. The impact should be more obvious if the students are placed under stress. This is related to a general hypothesis in psychology that specifies that under stress an organism will respond with the behavior appropriate to the situation that was learned first.[58] Consequently, Belkaoui tested the specific hypothesis that if a student learns two alternative responses to an informationg problem or stimulus and is placed under stress unrelated to the behavior being observed, he or she will respond to the stimulus with the first-learned method.[59] The results supported the hypothesis. Few implications of importance to the data-fixation hypothesis were made:

The appraisal of the usefulness of accounting technique cannot be ascertained when subjects are exposed to a stressful situation.

Given that stressful situations are likely to be present in both classroom and professional situations, there will be a predisposition to the use of the first learned accounting method.

Finally, the theoretical justifications pertaining to the choice of the appropriate accounting procedure by the firms can be reinforced by the learning order and the learning techniques to which the accountants have been exposed in their schools.[60]

The communication literature has addressed extensively the problem of the effects of order of presentation.[61] Known as the primacy-recency question, it is expressed by the following question: When both sides of a problem are presented successively, does the first-presented side (primacy) or the last-presented side (recency) have the advantage?

Different studies have supported the principle of primacy,[62] while other studies have created a controversy by reporting primacy effects under some conditions[63] and recency effects under others.[64] Consequently, Hovland, Jarvis, and Kelly recommended conducting research on the factors leading to the inconsistent effects of primacy and recency in the various experiments.[65] Examples of these factors include reinforcement, strength, involvement, and commitment. Ego involvement is also believed to be a variable that affects primacy and recency. Morteson noted:

Despite an absence of research, there is reason to believe that ego involvement may work against either primacy or recency, and often in a brutal way. Stated as a hypothesis, we may say that the more highly involved one is on a belief-discrepant topic, the less is the chance for either a primacy or recency effect.[66]

Belkaoui investigated the impact of the primacy and recency effects of ego involvement or commitment to one's stand on an accounting topic.[67] He reasoned that under conditions of ego involvement, the forces for reinforcement were likely to be particularly active and the impact of primacy or recency to be particularly passive. Subjects coming in contact with a stressful situation, in the form of resolving an accounting problem, would revert to the technique or the side of the message that was more clear or basic to them. The results of his experiments, which used accounting students, showed that the students under stress responded with the "accounting behavior" that was more clear or basic to them. In other words, in matters of ego involvement with an accounting technique just learned, subjects will give importance to what is perceived as relevant, significant, or meaningful. This could explain some of the data-fixation findings where the subjects have reverted either to the use of the first-learned method (primacy) or the second-learned method (recency), or to the method more clear or basic to their ego involvement.

PROBLEMS IN DATA-FIXATION RESEARCH

Several problems exist in the present state of data-fixation research.

1. Most studies have not distinguished between data fixation, with its focus on output, and functional fixation, with its focus on function. Research is needed on both concepts, as they provide insight into and represent different aspects of the behavior of decision makers.

2. Extrapolations made by information management researchers could contain serious flaws if the simple fact of ignorance is confused with the psychological phenomenon of functional fixation, especially since most of the subjects used have been students rather than actual decision makers. This was Pearson's main criticism of Ashton's study; Pearson claimed that the inability of the subjects to adjust their decision process was due entirely to ignorance.[68] This fact was explicitly recognized by Barnes and Webb when they stated: "It is our view that functional fixity and ignorance are separate phenomena and that in order to identify the former empirically, the absence of the latter needs to be insured."[69]

3. Fundamental evidence points to the fact that intelligence mitigates fixity. The point has been recognized both in the psychological[70] and the accounting experiments.[71] Again, Barnes and Webb have stated:

> It would appear that those who were not fixated were less concerned with financial matters than their colleagues, as they were more concerned with providing an intellectual stimulus for their staff. Two groups appear therefore: those who can see around "trivial" financial matters and are concerned with "high matters" and those

who are not. The implication again is that intelligence mitigates fixity.[72]

4. There are two methodologies in the functional-fixation research: (a) The "*one-object*" approach, where subjects are given an experimental task to perform and a novel or new way can be used in the solution. Fixity occurs when only a small number of solutions emerge from the group of subjects, for whom the usual function of an object is accentuated. (b) The "*two-objects*" approach, where subjects are given two objects and a control group is given the use of one of the objects. Functional fixation results from the tendency of the subjects to use that object in the critical problem whose function has not been accentuated. All the accounting studies have used the one-object approach, and therein lies a problem, which has been expressed by Flavell, Cooper, and Loisell:

> While functional fixedness in the first case is a matter of solution vs. non-solution..., it is, in the second case a matter of choice of objects or means for the solution of a comparatively simple problem. It is to be expected that the last method is the one that gives the purest measure of functional fixedness. In the first method a difficult problem is used and the non-solution of this problem may very well be attributed to other factors than functional fixation.[73]

Thus, there is a need for evidence from accounting research that uses the two-object approach.

5. Most information management research on data fixation has been concerned with whether fixity exists rather than why it exists. With the exception of the study by Haka, Friedman, and Jones, none of the accounting experiments has offered explanations about why fixity exists or has provided ways to remove it. In contrast, the psychological literature began to focus on its causes immediately after discovering the phenomenon. Removing fixation became the objective as experiments investigated factors such as time and the number of "other functions" shown for the fixated objects that affect the degree of fixity.[74] Later studies focused on the various ways of providing hints and cues to overcome fixation.[75] Needless to say, accounting research should now deal with the question of why fixity exists and how it can be mitigated. Wilner and Birnberg have stated the following to that effect:

> Despite the popularity among accounting researchers of the question of whether decision makers are fixated, the critical question would appear to be why at least a portion of decision makers exhibit fixation. Given that we know from various non-accounting studies that certain factors do inhibit creative problem analysis and solving, the role of accounting research should be to ascertain which of these inhibiting factors operate in the domain of accounting and to ascertain how we can reduce their detrimental effect.[76]

6. Wilner and Birnberg have pointed to the following problems in the design of existing studies on fixation:

1. The studies used an input-output methodology and the divergence between the inputs and the expected outputs were attributed to functional fixation while in fact there ma be other reasons why a subject fails to alter his information processing after an accounting change.

2. While random assignment of subjects to tasks is used to lessen the effects of individual differences, it still remains that it cannot overcome the systematic characteristics that prevent all subjects from understanding the task.

3. Most of the subjects used in these experiments are not sophisticated enough for the risks, which suggests that they were not fixated but rather naïve or ignorant.

4. Unlike the psychological experiments, which provided feedback to subjects, the accounting experiments not only did not provide any feedback, but used experimental tasks that were judgmental rather than optimal (right or wrong), which suggests that the subjects in the accounting experiments never knew if their behavior was appropriate.

5. Some knowledgeable subjects may have resisted changing their decision (model) following the accounting change for reasons other than fixation if (a) they viewed the change as irrelevant, (b) they viewed changing his decision process as not worthwhile in that it leads to a different action than that already performed, (c) they viewed the benefits of "better decision" as not outweighing the costs of learning how to process the change, (d) they thought it beneficial to act in a fixated manner

because of their double role as information senders as well as information users, and (e) possibly they formed a set that they could not overcome.[77]

ALTERNATIVE METHODOLOGY FOR DATA-FIXATION RESEARCH

Most of the empirical studies in data-fixation research have been based on laboratory or field experiments, with the exception of one single case based on a survey. In addition, with few exceptions, these experiments have used students as subjects, thereby raising problems of external validity. The tasks have not been realistic or motivating and have required judgmental rather than optimal behavior. What stands out upon review of the information management and psychological literature on the phenomenon is the urgent need for a better methodology, one that will allow direct observation of the process by which a decision is made. An appropriate methodology would be some form of protocol analysis, in which the subjects are asked to think aloud while solving the requirements of an experimental task. Such an approach would answer some very important questions.

1. Did the subject note the change?
2. Did the subject give any indication of appreciating its relevance?
3. Was the change understood?
4. Was the change ignored on grounds of its materiality, etc.?[78]

Better insights on the phenomenon of functional fixation may be possible through the use of protocol analysis, as the experiments use richer tasks, smaller pools of subjects, and better debriefing.

CONCLUSION

Functional fixation as observed in psychology and data fixation as observed in information management need to be better examined and explained. Future research should provide theoretical as well as empirical explanations of the reasons why subjects in accounting experiments persist in failing to adjust their decision process in response to accounting changes. In addition, richer and more realistic experimental tasks, sophisticated subjects, as well as protocol analysis ought to be used to provide better explanations of the phenomenon if it exists.

NOTES

1. N.R.F. Maier, "Reasoning in Humans: The Mechanisms of Equivalent Stimuli and Reasoning," *Journal of Experimental Psychology* (April 1945): 349-60.

2. K. Duncker, "On Problem Solving," *Psychological Monographs* 58, no. 5 (1945).

3. H.G. Birch and H.S. Rabinowitz, "The Negative Effect of Previous Experience on Productive Thinking," *Journal of Experimental Psychology* (February 1951): 121-25.

4. J.H. Flavell, A. Cooper, and R.H. Loisell, "Effect of the Number of Pre-utilization Functions on Functional Fixedness in Problem Solving," *Psychological Reports* (June 1958): 343-50.

5. R.E. Adamson, "Functional Fixedness as Related to Problem Solving: A Repetition of Three Experiments," *Journal of Experimental Psychology* (October 1952): 288-91.

6. Ibid., 288.

7. R.E. Adamson and D.W. Taylor, "Functional Fixedness as Related to Elapsed Time and to Set," *Journal of Experimental Psychology* (February 1954): 122-26.

8. S. Glucksberg and J.H. Danks, "Functional Fixedness: Stimulus Equivalence Mediated by Semantic-Acoustic Similarity," *Journal of Experimental Psychology* (July 1967): 400-405; J. Jensen, "On Functional Fixedness: Some Critical Remarks," *Scandinavian Journal of Psychology* (Winter 1960): 157-62.

9. Adamson and Taylor, "Functional Fixedness."

10. Duncker, "On Problem Solving."

11. P. Saugstad and K. Raaheim, "Problem Solving, Past Experience and Availability of Functions." *British Journal of Psychology* (May 1960): 97-104.

12. A. S. Luchins and E.H. Luchins, "New Experimental Attempts at Presenting Mechanization in Problem Solving," in *Thinking and Reasoning: Selected Reasings,* ed. P.C. Watson and P.N. Johnson Laird (Hammondsworth, Eng.: Penguin, 1968), 42-44.

13. Y. Ijiri, R.K. Jaedicke, and K.E. Knight, "The Effects of Accounting Alternatives on Management Decisions," in *Research in Accounting Measurement,* ed. R.K. Jaedicke, Y. Ijiri, and O. Nielsen (Sarasota, FL.: American Accounting Association, 1966), 186-99.

14. Ibid., 194.

15. Ibid., 194.

16. K.E. Knight, "Effect of Effort on Behavioral Rigidity in Luchins' Water Jar Task." *Journal of Abnormal and Social Psychology* (1960): 192-94; Paul Barnes and John Webb, "Management Information Changes and Functional Fixation: Some Experimental Evidence from the Public Sector," *Accounting, Organizations and Society* (February 1986): 1-18.

17. R.H. Ashton, "Cognitive Changes Induced by Accounting Changes: Experimental Evidence on the Functional Fixation Hypothesis," supplement to *Journal of Accounting Research* (1976): 1-17.

18. Ibid., 5.

19. Ibid., 1-7.

20. Robert Libby, "Discussion of Cognitive Changes Induced by Accounting Changes—Experimental Evidence on the Functional Fixation Hypothesis," supplement to *Journal of Accounting Research* (1976): 18-24.

21. Ibid., 23.

22. David B. Pearson, "Discussion of Cognitive Changes Induced by Accounting Changes—Experimental Evidence on the Functional Fixation Hypothesis," supplement to *Journal of Accounting Research* (1976): 25-28.

23. R.J. Swieringa, T.R. Dyckman, and R.E. Hoskin, "Empirical Evidence about the Effects of an Accounting Change on Information Processing," in *Behavioral Experiments in Accounting 11,* ed. T.J. Burns (Columbus: Ohio State University Press, 1979), 225-59.

24. T.R. Dyckman, R.E. Hoskin, and R.J. Swieringa, "An Accounting Change and Information Processing Changes," *Accounting, Organizations and Society* (February 1982): 1-11.

25. D.L. Chang and J.G. Birnberg, "Functional Fixity in Accounting Research: Perspective and New Data," *Journal of Accounting Research* (Autumn 1977): 300-312.

26. Ibid., 311.

27. R. A. Abdel-Khalik and T.F. Keller, "Earnings or Cash Flows: An Experiment on Functional Fixation and the Valuation of the Firm," *Studies in Accounting Research* 16 (Sarasota, FL,: American Accounting Association, 1979).

28. Ibid., 17.

29. Robert Bloom, Pieter T. Elgers, and Dennis Murray, "Functional Fixation in Product Pricing: A Comparison of Individuals and Groups," *Accounting, Organizations and Society* 9 no. 1 (1984): 1-11.

30. Ibid., 8.

31. Neil Wilner and Jacob Birnberg, "Methodological Problems in Functional Fixation Research: Criticism and Suggestions," *Accounting, Organizations and Society* (February 1986): 74.

32. Robert W. McGee. "Software Accounting, Bank Lending Decisions, and Stock Prices," *Management Accounting* (July 1984): 20-23.

33. Ibid., 20.

34. Ahmed Belkaoui, "Accrual Accounting, Modified Cash Basis of Accounting and the Loan Decision: An Experiment in Functional Fixation," unpublished manuscript, University of Illinois at Chicago, 1988.

35. Robert E. Jensen, "An Experimental Design for the Study of Effects of Accounting Variations in Decision Making," *Journal of Accounting Research* (Autumn 1966): 224-38.

36. J.L. Livingstone, "A Behavioral Study of Tax Allocation in Electric Utility Regulation," *The Accounting Review* (July 1967): 544-52.

37. Ibid., 550-51.

38. Ibid., 552.

39. F.A. Mlynarezyk, Jr., "An Empirical Study of Accounting Methods and Stock Prices," supplement to *Journal of Accounting Research* (1969(: 63-81.

40. W.H. Beaver, "The Behavior of Security Prices and Its Implications for Accounting Research Methods," supplement to *The Accounting Review* (1972): 407-37.

41. Ibid., 420-21.

42. Knight, "Effect of Effort on Behavioral Rigidity"; Barnes and Webb, "Management Information Changes and Functional Fixation."

43. Luchins and Luchins, "New Experimental Attempts."

44. J.A. Schumpeter, *Capitalism, Socialism and Democracy,* 3d ed. (New York: Harper & Row, 1950), 123-24.

45. Robert R. Sterling, "On Theory Construction and Verification," *The Accounting Review* (July 1970): 433.

46. L. Revsine, *Replacement Cost Accounting* (Englewood Cliffs, NJ: Prentice-Hall 1973), 50-51.

47. D. Kahneman and A. Tversky, "Prospect Theory: An Analysis of Decision under Risk," *Econometrika* (March 1979): 263-91.

48. Ibid., 265.

49. Ibid., 268.

50. Ibid., 271.

51. R. S. Woodworth and H. Schosberg, *Experimental Psychology* (New York: Henry Holt, 1954), 733.

52. Ibid.

53. G.E. Muller and F. Schumann, "Experimentelle Beitrage Zur Untersuchung de Gedachtnisses," *Zeischrift fur Psychologie* (1894): 81-190, 257-339.

54. A.C. Catania, *Learning* (Englewood Cliffs, NJ: Prentice-Hall, 1979).

55. J. Kagan and E. Havemann, *Psychology: An Introduction,* 3d ed. (New York: Harcourt Brace Jovanovich, 1976), 149.

56. Susan Haka, Lauren Friedman, and Virginia Jones, "Functional Fixation and Theoretical and Empirical Investigation," *The Accounting Review* (July 1986): 455-74.

57. Ibid., 460.

58. R.P. Barthol and Nari D. Ku, "Specific Regression under a Nonrelated Stress Situation," *American Psychologist* (February 1963): 482.

59. Ahmed Belkaoui, "Learning Order and the Acceptance of Accounting Techniques," *The Accounting Review* (October 1975): 897-99.

60. Ibid., 898-99.

61. C. Hovland, I. Jarvis, and H. Kelly, *Communication and Persuasion* (New Haven, CT: Yale University Press, 1953).

62. F.H. Lund, "The Psychology of Belief: IV. The Law of Primacy in Persuasion," *Journal of Abnormal and Social Psychology* (1925): 236-49; F.H. Kroner, "Experimental Studies of Changes in Altitudes: II. A study of the Effect of Printed Arguments on Changes in Attitudes," *Social Psychology* (1936): 522-32.

63. R.Lana, "Controversy on the Topic and the Order of Presentation in Persuasive Communications," *Psychological Reports* (April 1963): 163-70.

64. C.A. Insko, "Primacy versus Recency in Persuasion as a Function of the Timing of Arguments and Measurement," *Journal of Abnormal and Social Psychology* (1964): 381-91.

65. Hovland, Jarvis, and Kelly, *Communication and Persuasion.*

66. David C. Morteson, *Communication: The Study of Human Interaction* (New York: McGraw-Hill, 1972).

67. Ahmed Belkaoui, "The Primacy-Recency Effect, Ego Involvement and the Acceptance of Accounting Techniques," *The Accounting Review* (January 977): 252-56.

68. Pearson, "Discussion of Cognitive Changes Induced by Accounting Changes."

69. Barnes and Webb, "Management Information Changes and Functional Fixation."

70. Luchins and Luchins, "New Experimental Attempts."

71. Barnes and Webb, "Management Information Changes and Functional Fixation."

72. Ibid., 12.

73. Flavell, Cooper, and Loisell, "Effect of the Number of Pre-utilization Functions."

74. Adamson and Taylor, "Functional Fixedness"; Flavell, Cooper, and Loisell, "Effect of the Number of PreOutilization Functions."

75. N.A. Wilner and J.G. Birnberg, "A Comparison of the Accoutning and Psychological Literature on Functional Fixation," unpublished working paper, University of Pittsburgh, 1984.

76. N.A. Wilner and J.G. Birnberg, "Methodological Problems in Functional Fixation Research: Criticisms and Suggestions," *Accounting, Organizations and Society* (February 1986): 75.

77. Ibid., 75-78.

78. Ibid., 78-79.

SELECTED BIBLIOGRAPHY

Adamson, R.E. "Functional Fixation as Related to Problem Solving: A Repetition of Three Experiments." *Journal of Experimental Psychology* (October 1952): 288-91.

Adamson, R.E., and D.W. Taylor. "Functional Fixedness as Related to Elapsed Time and to Set." *Journal of Experimental Psychology* (February 1954): 122-126.

Ausubel, D., L.C. Robbins, and E. Blake. "Retroactive Inhibition and Facilitation in the Learning of School Materials." *Journal of Educational Psychology* (October 1957): 334-43.

Belkaoui, Ahmed. "Accrual Accounting, Modified Cash Basis of Accounting and the Loan Decision: An Experiment in Functional Fixation." Unpublished manuscript, University of Illinois at Chicago, 1988.

———. "Learning Order and the Acceptance of Accounting Techniques." *The Accounting Review* (October 1975): 897-99.

———. "The Primacy-Recency Effect, Ego Involvement and the Acceptance of Accounting Techniques." *Accounting Review* (January 1977): 252-56.

Birch, H.G., and H.S. Rabinowitz. "The Negative Effect of Previous Experience on Productive Thinking." *Journal of Experimental Psychology* (February 1951): 121-25.

Catania, A.C. *Learning.* Englewood Cliffs, NJ: Prentice-Hall, 1979.

Duncker, K. "On Problem Solving." *Psychological Monographs* 58, no. 5 (1945).

Dyckman, T.R., M. Gibbins, and R.J. Swieringa. "Experimental and Survey Research in Financial Accounting: A Review and Evaluation." In *The Impact of Accounting Research on Practice and Disclosure,* ed. A.R. Abdel-Khalik and T.T. Relier, Durham, NC: Duke University Press, 1978, 48-105.

Flavell, J.H., A. Cooper, and R.H. Loisell. "Effect of the Number of Pre-utilization Functions on Functional Fixedness in Problem Solving." *Psychological Reports* (June 1958): 343-50.

Glucksberg, S., and J.H. Danks. "Functional Fixedness: Stimulus Equivalence Mediated by Semantic-Acoustic Similarity." *Journal of Experimental Psychology* (July 1967): 400-405.

Hoch, S.J. "Availability and Interference in Predictive Judgments." Working paper, Center for Decision Research, Graduate School of Business, University of Chicago, March 1984.

Hovland, C., I. Jarvis, and H. Kelly. *Communication and Persuasion.* New Haven, CT: Yale University Press, 1953.

Insko, C.A. "Primacy versus Recency in Persuasion as a Function of the Timing of Argument and Measurement." *Journal of Abnormal and Social Psychology* (1964): 381-91.

Jensen, J. "On Functional Fixedness: Some Critical Remarks." *Scandinavian Journal of Psychology* (Winter 1960): 157-62.

Kagan, J., and E. Havemann. *Psychology: An Introduction,* 3d ed. New York: Harcourt Brace Jovanovich, 1976.

Kahneman, D., and A. Tversky. "Prospect Theory: An Analysis of Decision under Risk." *Econometrika* (March 1979): 263-91.

Knight, K.E. "Effect of Effort on Behavioral Rigidity in Luchins' Water Jar Task." *Journal of Abnormal and Social Psychology* (1960): 192-94.

Krowner, F.H. "Experimental Studies of Changes in Attitudes: II. A Study of the Effect of Printed Arguments on Changes in Attitudes." *Social Psychology* (1936): 522-32.

Lana, R. "Controversy on the Topic and the Order of Presentation in Persuasive Communications." *Psychological Reports* (April 1963): 163-70.

Larcker, D.F., and V.P. Lessig. "Perceived Usefulness of Information: A Psychometric Examination." *Decision Sciences* (January 1980): 121-34.

Luchins, A.S., and E.H. Luchins. "New Experimental Attempts at Presenting Mechanization in Problem Solving." In *Thinking and Reasoning: Selected Readings,* ed. P.C. Watson and P.N. Johnson Laird. Hammondsworth, Eng.: Penguin, 1968, 42-44.

Lund, F.H. "The Psychology of Belief: IV. The Law of Primacy in Persuasion." *Journal of Abnormal and Social Psychology* (1925): 236-49.

Martin, E. "Verbal Learning Theory and Independent Retrieval Phenomena." *Psychological Review* (July 1971): 314-32.

Mehle, T., C.F. Gettys, C. Manning, S. Baca, and S. Fisher. "The Availability Explanation Plausibility Assessment." *Acta Psychologica* (November 1981): 127-40.

Morteson, David C. *Communication: The Study of Human Interaction.* New York: McGraw-Hill, 1972.

Muller, G.E., and F. Schumann. "Experimentelle Bertrage Zur Untersuchung de Gedachtnisses." *Zeitschrift fur Psychologie* (1894): 81-190, 257-339.

Roediger, H.L. "Recall as a Self-Limiting Process." *Memory and cognition* (January 1978): 54-63.

Saugstad, P, and K. Raaheim. "Problem Solving, Past Experience and Availability of Functions." *British Journal of Psychology* (May 1960): 97-104.

Sherif, C.W., and M. Sherif. *Attitude, Ego Involvement, and Change.* New York: Wiley, 1967.

Sherif, M., and C.I. Hovland. *Social Judgement: Assimilation and Contrast Effects and Attitude Change.* New Haven, CT: Yale University Press, 1961.

Sterling, Robert R. "Accounting Research, Education and Practice." *Journal of Accountancy* (September 1973): 44-52.

———. " A Case of Valuation and Learned Cognitive Dissonance." *Journal of Accounting Review* (April 1967): 376-78.

———. *Theory of Measurement of Enterprise Income.* Lawrence, TX: Scholars Book Co., 1970.

Tversky, A. "Features of Similarity." *Psychological Review* (July 1977): 327-52.

Tversky, A., and D. Kahneman. "The Framing of Decisions and the Psychology of Choice." *Science* (January 1981): 453-58.

Wong, M. "Retroactive Inhibition in Meaningful Verbal Learning." *Journal of Educational Psychology* (October 1970): 410-15.

Woodworth, R.S., and H. Schosberg. *Experimental Psychology,* rev. ed. New York: Henry Holt, 1954.

6. PLANNING, BUDGETING, AND INFORMATION DISTORTION

INTRODUCTION

In both the process of planning and budgeting, managers may be tempted to distort the information in a process better known as slack behavior. Richard M. Cyert and James G. March advanced the concept of organizational slack as a hypothetical construct to explain overall organizational phenomena.1 Arie Y. Lewin and Carl Wolf, on the other hand, have made the following warning: "Slack is a seductive concept; it 'explains' too much and predicts' too little."[2] Indeed, slack research needs to be categorized along more precise dimensions that better explain its nature and its impact. Accordingly, this chapter reviews the on slack by differentiating between *organizational slack and budgetary slack*.

VIEWS OF SLACK

Slack arises from the tendency of organizations and individuals to refrain from using all the resources available to them. It describes a tendency not to operate at peak efficiency. In general, two types of slack have been identified in the literature, organizational slack and budgetary slack. Organizational slack basically refers to an unused capacity, in the sense that the demands put on the resources of the organization are less than the supply of these resources. Budgetary slack is found in the budgetary process and refers to the intentional distortion of information that results from an understatement of budgeted sales and an overstatement of budgeted costs.

The concepts of organizational slack and budgetary slack appear in other literature under different labels. Economists refer to an X-inefficiency in instances where resources are either not used to their full capacity or effectiveness or are used in an extremely wasteful manner, as well as in instances where managers fail to make costless improvements. X-inefficiency is to be differentiated from allocative inefficiency, which refers to whether or not prices in a market are of the right kind, that is, whether they allocate input and output to whose users who are willing to pay for them.[3] Categories of inefficiency of a nonallocative nature, or X-inefficiency, include inefficiency in (1) labor utilization, (2) capital utilization, (3) time sequence, (4) extent of employee cooperation, (5) information flow, (6) bargaining effectiveness, (7) credit availability utilization, and (8) heuristic procedures.[4]

Agency theory also refers to slack behavior. The problem addressed by the agency theory literature is how to design an incentive contract such that the total gains can be maximized, given (1) information asymmetry between principal and agent, (2) pursuit of self-interest by the agent, and (3) environmental uncertainty affecting the outcome of the agent's decisions.[5] Slack can occur when managers dwell in an "excess consumption of perquisites" or in a "tendency to shrink." Basically, slack is the possible "shrinking" behavior of an agent.[6]

The literature in organizational behavior refers to slack in terms of defensive, tactical responses and deceptive behavior. By viewing organizations as political environments, the deceptive aspects of individual power-acquisition behavior become evident.[7] A variety of unobtrusive tactics in the operation of power,[8] covert intents and means of those exhibiting power-acquisition behaviors,[9] and a "wolf in sheep's clothing" phenomenon, whereby individuals profess a mission or goal strategy while practicing an individual-maximization strategy,[10] characterize these deceptive behaviors, which are desired to present an illusionary or false impression. V.E. Schein has provided the following examples of deceptive behaviors in communication, decision making, and presentation of self.

Communication. With regard to written or oral communications, there may be an illusion that these communications include all the information or that these communications are true, which masks the reality either of their consisting of only partial information or of their actually distorting the information.

Decision making. A manager may present the illusion that he or she is actually compromising or giving in with regard to a decision, whereas in reality he or she is planning to lose this particular battle with the long-range objective of winning the war. Or a manager or a subunit may initiate a particular action and then work on plans and activities for implementing a program. This intensive planning and studying, however, may in reality be nothing more than a delaying tactic, during which the actual program will die or be forgotten. Underlying this illusion that one is selecting subordinates, members of boards of directors, or successors on the basis of their competence may be the reality that these individuals are selected for loyalty, compliance, or conformity to the superior's image.

Presentation of self. Many managers exude an apparent confidence, when in reality they are quite uncertain. Still other managers are skilled in organizing participatory group decision-making sessions, which in reality have been set up to produce a controlled outcome.[11]

Schein then hypothesized that the degree to which these behaviors are deceptive seems to be a function of both the nature of the organization and of the kinds of power exhibited (work-related or personal)[12]. She relied on Cyert and March's dichotomization of organizations as either low- or high-slack systems.[13] Low-slack systems are characterized by a highly competitive environment that requires rapid and nonroutine decision making on the part of its members and a high level of productive energy and work outcomes to secure an effective performance. High-slack systems are characterized by a reasonably stable environment that requires routine decision making to secure an effective performance. Given these dichotomizations, Schein suggested that:

1. The predominant form of power acquisition behavior is personal in a high-slack organization and work-related in a low-slack organization.
2. The underlying basis of deception is the inherently overt nature of personal power acquisition behaviors in a

high-slack organization and an organization's illusion as to how work gets done in a low-slack organization.

3. The benefits of deception to members are the provisions of excitement and personal rewards in a high-slack organization and the facilitation of work accomplishment and organizational rewards in a low-slack organization.

4. The benefits of deception to organization are to foster [the] illusion of a fast-paced, competitive environment in a high-slack organization and to maintain an illusion of workability of the formal structure in a low-slack organization.[14]

ORGANIZATIONAL SLACK

Nature of Organizational Slack

There is no lack of definitions for organizational slack, as can be seen from the definitions provided by Cyert and March,[15] Child,[16] Cohen, March, and Olsen,[17] March and Olsen,[18] Dimmick and Murray,[19] Litschert and Bonham,[20] and March.[21]

What appears from these definitions is that organizational slack is a buffer created by management in its use of available resources to deal with internal as well as external events that may arise and threaten an established coalition. Slack, therefore, is used by management as an agent of change in response to changes in both the internal and external environments.

Cyert and March's model explains slack in terms of cognitive and structural factors.[22] It provides the rationale for the unintended creation of slack. Individuals are assumed to "satisfice," in the sense that they set aspiration levels for performance rather than a maximization goal. These aspirations adjust upward or downward, depending on actual performance, and in a slower fashion than actual changes in performance. This lag in adjustment allows excess resources from superior performance to accumulate in the form of an organizational stabilizing force to absorb excess resources in good times without requiring a revision of aspirations and intentions regarding the use of these excess resources. "By absorbing excess resources it retards upward adjustment of aspirations during relatively good times…by providing a pool of emergency resources, it permits aspirations to be maintained during relatively bad times."[23]

Oliver E. Williamson has proposed a model of slack based on managerial incentives.[24] This model provides the rationale for managers' motivation and desire for slack resources. Under conditions where managers are able to pursue their own objectives, the model predicts that the excess resources available after target levels of profit have been reached are not allocated according to profit-maximization rules. Organizational slack becomes the means by which a manager achieves his or her personal goals, as characterized by four motives: income, job security, status, and discretionary control over resources. Williamson makes the assumption that the manager is motivated to maximize his or her personal goals subject to satisfying organizational objectives and that the manager achieves this by maximizing slack resources under his or her control. Williamson has suggested that there are four levels of profits: (1) a maximizing profit equal to the profit that the firm would achieve when marginal revenue equals marginal cost, (2) actual profit equal to the true profit achieved by the firm, (3) reported profit equal to the accounting profit reported in the annual report, and (4) minimum profit equal to the profit needed to maintain the organizational coalition. If the market is noncompetitive, various forms of slack emerge: (1) *slack absorbed as staff* equal to the difference between maximum and actual profit, (2) *slack in the form of cost* equal to the difference between reported and minimum profits, and (3) *discretionary spending for investment* equal to the difference between reported and minimum profits.

Income smoothing can be used to substantiate the efforts of management to neutralize environmental uncertainty and to create organizational slack by means of an accounting manipulation of the level of earnings. J.Y. Kamin and J. Ronen have related organizational slack to income smoothing by reasoning that what often results in slack accumulation is aimed at smoothing earnings.[25] They hypothesized that management-controlled firms were more likely to be engaged in smoothing as a manifestation of managerial discretion and slack. "Accounting" and "real" smoothing were tested by observing the behavior of discretionary expenses vis-à-vis the behavior of income numbers. Their results showed that (1) a majority of the firms behaved as if they were income smoothers and (2) a particularly strong majority was found among management-controlled firms with high barriers to entry. This line of reasoning was pursued by Ahmed Belkaoui and R.D. Picur.[26] Their study tested the effects of the dual economy on income-smoothing behavior. It was hypothesized that a higher degree of smoothing of income numbers would be exhibited by firms in the periphery sector than by firms in the core sector in reaction to different opportunity structures and experiences. Their results indicated that a majority of the firms may have been resorting to income smoothing. A higher number were found among firms in the periphery sector.

Lewin and Wolf proposed the following statements as a theoretical framework for understanding the concept of slack:

1. Organizational slack depends on the availability of excess resources.
2. Excess resources occur when an organization generates or has the potential to generate resources in excess of what is necessary to maintain the organizational coalition.
3. Slack occurs unintentionally as a result of the imperfection of the resource allocation decision-making process.
4. Slack is created intentionally because managers are motivated to maximize slack resources under their control to ensure achievement of personal goals subject to the achievement of organizational goals.
5. The disposition of slack resources is a function of a manager's expense preference function.
6. The distribution of slack resources is an outcome of the bargaining process-setting organization and reflects the discretionary power of organization members in allocating resources.
7. Slack can be present in a distributed or concentrated form.

8. The aspiration of organizational participants for slack adjusts upward as resources become available. The downward adjustment of aspirations for slack resources, when resources become scarce, is resisted by organizational participants.

9. Slack can stabilize short-term fluctuations in the firm's performance.

10. Beyond the short term, the reallocation of slack requires a change in organizational goals.

11. Slack is directly related to organizational size, maturity, and stability of the external environment.[27]

Functions of Organizational Slack

Because the definition of slack is often intertwined with a description of the functions that slack serves, L.J. Bourgeois discussed these functions as a means of making palpable the ways of measuring slack.[28] From a review of the administrative theory literature, he identified organizational slack as an independent variable that either "causes" or serves four primary functions: "(1) as an inducement for organizational actors to remain in the system, (2) as a resource for conflict resolution, (3) as a buffering mechanism in the work flow process, or (4) as a facilitator of certain types of strategic or creative behavior within the organization."[29]

The concept of slack as an inducement to maintain the coalition was first introduced by C.I. Barnard in his treatment of the inducement/contribution ratio (VC) as a way of attracting organizational participants and sustaining their membership.[30] March and H.A. Simon later described slack resources as the source of inducements through which the inducement/contribution ratio might exceed a value of 1, which is equivalent to paying an employee more than would be required to retain his or her services.[31] This concept of slack was then explicitly introduced by Cyert and March as consisting of payments to members of the coalition in excess of what is required to maintain the organization.[32]

Slack as a resource for conflict resolution was introduced in L.R. Pondy's goal model.[33] In this model subunit goal conflicts are resolved partly by sequential attention to goals and partly by adopting a decentralized organizational structure. A decentralized structure is made possible by the presence of organizational slack.

A notion of slack as a technical buffer from the variances and discontinuities caused by environmental uncertainty was proposed by J.D. Thompson.[34] It was also acknowledged in Pondy's system model, which described conflict as a result of the lack of buffers between interdependent parts of an organization.[35] Jay Galbraith saw buffering as an information-processing problem: "Slack resources are an additional cost to the organization or the customer... The creation of slack resources, through reduced performance levels, reduces the amount of information that must be processed during task execution and prevents the overloading of hierarchical channels."[36]

According to Bourgeois, slack facilitates three types of strategic or creative behavior within the organization: (1) providing resources for innovative behavior, (2) providing opportunities for a satisficing behavior, and (3) affecting political behavior.[37]

First, as a facilitator of innovative behavior, slack tends to create conditions that allow the organization to experiment with new strategies[38] and introduce innovation.[39] Second, as a facilitator of suboptimal behavior, slack defines the threshold of acceptability of a choice, or "bounded search,"[40] by people whose bounded rationality leads them to satisfice.[41] Third, the notion that slack affects political activity was advanced by Cyert and March, who argued that slack reduces both political activity and the need for bargaining and coalition-forming activity.[42] Furthermore, W.G. Astley has argued that slack created by success results in self-aggrandizing behavior by managers who engage in political behavior to capture more than their fair share of the surplus.[43]

W. Richard Scott argued that lowered standards create slack—unused resources—that can be used to create ease in the system.[44] Notice the following comment: "Of course, some slack in the handling of resources is not only inevitable but essential to smooth operations. All operations require a margin of error to allow for mistakes, waste, spoilage, and similar unavoidable accompaniments of work."[45] But the inevitability of slack is not without consequences:

> The question is not whether there is to be slack but how much slack is permitted. Excessive slack resources increase costs for the organization that are likely to be passed on to the consumer. Since creating slack resources is a relatively easy and painless solution available to organizations, whether or not it is employed is likely to be determined by the amount of competition confronting the organization in its task environment.[46]

Measurement of Organizational Slack

One problem in investing empirically in the presence of organizational slack relates to the difficulty of securing an adequate measurement of the phenomenon. Various methods have been suggested. In addition to these methods, eight variables that appear in public data, whether they are created by managerial actions or made available by environment, may explain a change in slack.[47] The model, suggested by Bourgeois, is as follows:

Slack = f(RE, DP, G&A, WC/S, D/E, CR, I/P, P/E)

where

RE = Retained earnings

DP = Dividend payout

G&A = General and administrative expense

WC/S = Working capital as a percentage of sales

D/E = Debt as a percentage of equity

CR = Credit rating

I/P = Short-term loan interest compared to prime rate

P/E = Price/earnings ratio

Here RE, G&A, WC/S, and CR are assumed to have a positive effect on changes and DP, D/E, P/E, and I/P are assumed to have a negative effect on changes in slack.

Some of these measures have also been suggested by other researchers. For example, Martin M. Rosner used profit and excess capacity as slack measures,[48] and Lewin and Wolf used selling, general, and administrative expenses as surrogates for slack.[49] Bourgeois and Jitendra V. Singh refined these measures by suggesting that slack could be differentiated on an "ease-of-recovery" dimension.[50] Basically, they considered excess liquidity to be a available slack, not yet earmarked for particular uses. Overhead costs were termed recoverable slack, in the sense that they are absorbed by various organizational functions but can be recovered when needed elsewhere. In addition, the ability of a firm to generate resources from the environment, such as the ability to raise additional debt or equity capital, was considered *potential slack*. All of these measures were divided by sales to control for company size.

Building on Bourgeois and Singh's suggestions, Theresa K. Lant opted for the four following measures:

1. Administrative slack = (General and administrative expenses)/cost of goods sold
2. Available Liquidity = (Cash + Marketable Securities – Current Liabilities)/Sales

3. Recoverable Liquidity = (Accounts Receivable + Inventory)/Sales

4. Retained Earnings = (Net Profit – Dividends)/Sales[51]

Lant used these measures to show empirically (1) that available liquidity and general and administrative expenses have significantly higher variance than profit across firms and across time and (2) that the mean change in slack is significantly greater than the mean change in profit. She concluded as follows:

> These results are logically consistent with the theory that slack absorbs variance in actual profit. They also suggest that the measures used are reasonable measures for slack. Thus, it supports prior work which has used these measures and implies that further large sample models using slack as a variable are feasible since financial information is readily available for a large number of firms. Before these results can be generalized however, the tests conducted here should be replicated using different samples of firms from a variety of industries.[52]

BUDGETARY SLACK

Nature of Budgetary Slack

The literature on organizational slack shows that managers have the motives necessary to desire to operate in a slack environment. The literature on budgetary slack considers the budget as the embodiment of that environment and, therefore, assumes that managers will use the budgeting process to bargain for slack budgets. As stated by Michael Schiff and Lewin, "managers will create slack in budgets through a process of *understating revenues and overstating costs*."[53] The general definition of budgetary slack, then, is the understatement of revenues and the overstatement of costs in the budgeting process. A detailed description of the creation of budgetary slack by managers was reported by Schiff and Lewin in their study of the budget process of three divisions of multidivision companies.[54] They found evidence of budgetary slack through underestimation of gross revenue, inclusion of discretionary increases in personnel requirements, establishment of marketing and sales budgets with internal limits on funds to be spent, use of manufacturing costs based on standard costs that do not reflect process improvements operationally available at the plant, and inclusion of discretionary " special projects."

Evidence of budgetary slack has also been reported by others. A.E. Lowe and R.W. Shaw found a downward bias, introduced through sales forecasts by line managers, which assumed good performance where rewards were related to forecasts.[55] M. Dalton reported various examples of department managers' allocating resources to what they considered justifiable purposes, even though such purposes were not authorized in their budgets.[56] G. Shillinglaw noted the extreme vulnerability of budgets used to measure divisional performance given the great control exercised by divisional management in budget preparation and the reporting of results.[57]

Slack creation is a generalized organizational phenomenon. Many different organizational factors have been used to explain slack creation, in particular, organizational structure, goal congruence, control system, and managerial behavior. Slack creation is assumed to occur in cases where a Tayloristic organizational structure exists,[58] and it is also assumed to occur in a participative organizational structure.[59] It may be due to conflicts that arise between the individual and organizational goals, leading managers intentionally to create slack. It may also be due to the attitudes of management toward the budget and to worst views of the budgets as a device used by management to manipulate them.[60] Finally, the creation of slack may occur whether or not the organization is based on a centralized or decentralized structure.[61] With regard to this last issue, Schiff and Lewin have reported that the divisional controller appears to have undertaken the tasks of creating and managing divisional slack and is most influential in the internal allocation of slack.

Budgeting and the Propensity to Create Budgetary Slack

The budgeting system has been assumed to affect a manager's propensity to create budgetary slack, in the sense that this propensity can be increased or decreased by the way in which the budgeting system is designed or complemented. Mohamed Onsi was the first to investigate empirically the connections between the type of budgeting system and the propensity to create budgetary slack.[62] From a review of the literature, he stated the following four assumptions:

1. Managers influence the budget process through bargaining for slack by understating revenues and overstating costs.
2. Managers build up slack in "good years" and reconvert slack into profit in "bad years."
3. Top management is at a "disadvantage" in determining the magnitude of slack.
4. The divisional controller in decentralized organizations participates in the task of creating and managing divisional slack.[63]

Personal interviews of thirty-two managers of five large national and international companies and statistical analysis of a questionnaire were used to identify the important behavioral variables that influence slack buildup and utilization. The questionnaire's variables were grouped into the following eight dimensions;

1. *Slack attitude* described by the variables indicating a manager's attitude to slack.
2. *Slack manipulation* described by the variables indicating how a manager builds up and uses slack.
3. *Slack institutionalization* described by the variables that make a manager less inclined to reduce his or her slack.

4. *Slack detections* described by the variables indicating the superior's ability to detect slack based on the amount of information that he receives.

5. *Attitude toward the top management control system* described by the variables indicating an authoritarian philosophy toward budgeting being attributed to top management by divisional managers.

6. *Attitudes toward the divisional control system* described by variables on attitudes toward subordinates, sources of pressure, budget autonomy, budget participation, and supervisory uses of budgets.

7. *Attitudes toward the budget* described by variables on attitude toward the level of standards, attitude toward the relevancy of budget attainment to valuation of performance, and the manager's attitude (positive or negative) toward the budgetary system in general, as a managerial tool.

8. *Budget relevancy* described by variables indicating a manager's attitudes toward the relevancy of standards for his department's operation.[64]

Factor analysis reduced these dimensions to seven factors and showed a relationship between budgetary slack and what Onsi called "an authoritarian top management budgetary control system." Thus, he stated: "Budgetary slack is created as a result of pressure and the use of budgeted profit attainment as a basic criterion in evaluating performance. Positive participation could encourage less need for building up slack. However, the middle managers' perception of pressure was an overriding concern. The positive correlation between managers' attitudes and attainable level of standards is a reflection of this pressure."[65]

Cortland Cammann explored the moderating effects of subordinates' participation in decision making and the difficulty of subordinates' jobs based on their responses to different uses of control systems by their superiors.[66] His results showed that the use of control systems for contingent reward allocation produced defensive responses by subordinates under all conditions, which included the creation of budgetary slack. Basically, when superiors used budgeting information as a basis for allocating organizational rewards, their subordinates' responses were defensive. Allowing participation in the budget processes reduced this defensiveness.

Finally, Kenneth A. Merchant conducted a field study designed to investigate how managers' propensities to create budgetary slack are affected by the budgeting system and the technical context.[67] He hypothesized that the propensity to create budgetary slack is positively related to the importance placed on meeting budget targets and negatively related to the extent of participation allowed in budgeting processes, the degree of predictability in the production process, and the superiors' abilities to create slack. Unlike earlier studies drawn across functional areas, 170 manufacturing managers responded to a questionnaire measuring the propensity to create slack, the importance of meeting the budget, budget participation, the nature of technology in terms of work-flow integration and product standardization, and the ability of superiors to detect slack. The results suggested that managers' propensities to create slack (1) do vary with the setting and with how the budgeting system is implemented; (2) are lower where managers actively participate in budgeting, particularly when technologies are relatively predictable; and (3) are higher when a tight budget requires frequent tactical responses to avoid overruns.

The three studies by Onsi, Cammann, and Merchant provide evidence that participation may lead to positive communication between managers so that subordinates feel less pressure to create slack. This result is, in fact, contingent on the amount of information asymmetry existing between the principals (superiors) and the agents (the subordinates). Although participation in budgeting leads subordinates to communicate or reveal some of their private information, agents may still misrepresent or withhold some of their private information, leading to budgetary slack. Accordingly, Alan S. Dunk proposed a link between participation and budgetary slack through two variables: superiors' budget emphasis in their evaluation of subordinate performance and the degree of information asymmetry between superiors and subordinates:[68] "When participation, budget emphasis, and information asymmetry are high (low), slack will be high (low)."[69] The results, however, showed that low (high) slack is related to high (low) participation, budget emphasis, and information asymmetry. The results are stated as follows: The results of this study show that the relation between participation and slack is contingent upon budget emphasis and information asymmetry, but in a direction contrary to expectations.

> The results provide evidence for the utility of participative budgeting, and little support for the view that high participation may result in increased slack when the other two predictors are high. Although participation may induce subordinates to incorporate slack in budgets, the results suggest that participation alone may not be sufficient. The findings suggest that slack reduction results from participation, except when budget emphasis is low.[70]

Budgetary Slack, Information Distortion, and Truth-Inducing Incentive Schemes

Budgetary slack involves a deliberate distortion of input information. Distortion of input information in a budget setting arises, in particular, from the need of managers to accommodate their expectations about the kinds of payoffs associated with different possible outcomes. Several experiments have provided evidence of such distortion of input information. Cyert, March, and W.H. Starbuck showed in a laboratory experiment that subjects adjusted the information that they transmitted in a complex decision-making system to control their payoffs.[71] Similarly, Lowe and Shaw have shown that in cases where rewards were linked to forecasts, sales managers tended to distort the input information and to induce biases in their sales forecast.[72] Dalton also provided some rich situational descriptions of information distortion in which lower-level managers distorted the budget information and allocated resources to what were perceived to be justifiable objectives.[73] Finally, a payoff structure can induce a forecaster to bias intentionally his or her forecast. R.M. Barefield provided a model of forecast behavior that showed a "rough" formulation of a possible link between a forecaster's biasing and the quality of the forecaster as a resource of data for an accounting system.[74]

Taken together, these studies suggest that budgetary slack, through systematic distortion of input information, can be used to accommodate the subjects' expectations about the payoffs associated with various possible outcomes. They fail, however, to provide a convincing rationalization of the link between distortion of input information and the subjects' accommodation of their expectations. Agency theory and issues related to risk aversion may provide such a lin. Hence, given the existence of divergent incentives and information asymmetry between the controller (or employer) and the controlee (or employee) and the high cost of observing employee skill or effort, a budget-based employment contract (i.e., where employee compensation is contingent on meeting the performance standard) can be Pareto-superior to fixed pay or linear sharing rules (where the employer and employee split the output).[75] However, these budget-based schemes impose a risk on the employee, as job performance can be affected by a host of uncontrollable factors. Consequently, risk-averse individuals may resort to slack budgeting through systematic distortion of input information. In practice, moreover, any enhanced (increased) risk aversion would lead the employee to resort to budgetary slack. One might hypothesize that, without proper incentives for truthful communication, the slack budgeting behavior could be reduced. One suggested avenue is the use of truth-inducing, budget-based schemes.[76] These schemes, assuming risk neutrality, motivate a worker to reveal truthfully private information about future performance and to maximize performance regardless of the budget.

Accordingly, Mark S. Young conducted an experiment to test the effects of risk aversion and asymmetric information on slack budgeting.[77] Five hypotheses related to budgetary slack were developed and tested using a laboratory experiment. The hypotheses were as follows:

> Hypothesis 1: A subordinate who participates in the budgeting process will build slack into the budget...
>
> Hypothesis 2: A risk-aversion subordinate will build in more budget slack than a non-risk-averse subordinate...
>
> Hypothesis 3: Social pressure not to misrepresent productive capability will be greater for a subordinate whose information is known by management than for a subordinate having private information...
>
> Hypothesis 4: As social pressure increases for the subordinate, there is a lower degree of budgetary slack...
>
> Hypothesis 5: A subordinate who has private information builds more slack into the budget than a subordinate whose information is known by management.[78]

The results of the experiment confirmed the hypotheses that a subordinate who participates builds in budgetary slack and that slack is, in part, attributable to a subordinate's risk preferences. Given state uncertainty and a worker-manager information asymmetry about performance capability, the subjects in the experiment created slack even in the presence of a truth-inducing scheme. In addition, risk-averse workers created more slack than non-risk-averse workers did. Similarly, C. Chow, J. Cooper, and W. Waller provided evidence that, given a worker-manager information asymmetry about performance capability, slack is lower under a truth-inducing scheme than under a budget-based scheme with an incentive to create slack.[79]

Both Young's and Chow, Cooper, and Waller's studies were found to have limitations.[80] With regard to Young's study, William S. Waller found three limitations: "First, unlike the schemes examined in the analytical research, the one used in his study penalized outperforming the budget, which limits its general usefulness. Second, there was no manipulation of incentives, so variation in slack due to incentives was not examined. Third, risk preferences were measured using the conventional lottery technique of which the validity and reliability are suspect."[81] With regard Chow, Cooper, and Waller's study, Waller found the limitations to be the assumption of state certainly and the failure to take risk preference into account. Accordingly, Waller conducted an experiment under which subjects participatively set budgets under either a scheme with an incentive for creating slack or a truth-incentive scheme like those examined in the analytical research. In addition, risk neutrality was induced for one-half of the subjects, and constant, absolute risk aversion for the rest, using a technique discussed by J. Berg, L. Daley, J. Dickhaut, and T. O'Brien that allows the experimenter to induce (derived) utility functions with any shape.[82] The results of the experiment show that when a conventional truth-inducing scheme is introduced, slack decreases for risk-neutral subjects but not for risk-averse subjects. Added to the evidence provided by the other studies, this study indicates that risk preference is an important determinant of slack, especially in the presence of a truth-inducing scheme.

Basically, there is preliminary evidence that risk-averse workers create more budgetary slack than risk-neutral ones. In addition, "truth-inducing incentive schemes" reduce budgetary slack for risk-neutral subjects but not for risk-averse subjects. It seems that resource allocations within organizations are mediated by perceptions of risk, where risk is a stable personal trait. Accordingly, D.C. Kim tested whether risk preferences are domain-specific, that is, whether latent risk preferences translate into differing manifest risk preferences according to the context.[83] He relied on an experiment simulating the public accountants' budgeting of billable bonus to test the hypothesis that subject preference for tight or safe budget behavior depends on the performance of coworkers and domain-specific risk preferences. The results supported the view that subordinates' risk preferences are influenced by a situation-dependent variable. As stated by Kim: "The reversal of risk preferences around a neutral reference point is statistically significant for both dispositionally risk-averse and dispositionally risk-seeking subjects. The dispositional variable also contributes to the explanation of variations in subjects' manifest risk preferences. Thus the propensity to induce budgetary slack seems to be a joint function of situations and dispositions."[84]

Budgetary Slack and Self-Esteem

The enhancement of risk aversion and the resulting distortion of input information can be more pronounced when self-esteem is threatened. It was found that persons who have low opinions of themselves are more likely to cheat than persons with higher self-esteem.[85] A situation of dissonance was created in an experimental group by giving out positive feedback about a personality test to some participants and negative feedback to others. All of the participants were then asked to take part in a competitive game of cards. The participants who received a blow to their self-esteem cheated more often than those who had received positive feedback about themselves. Could it also be concluded that budgetary slack through information distortion may be a form of dishonest behavior, arising from the enhancement of risk aversion caused by a negative feedback on self-esteem? A person's expectations can be an important determinant of his or her behavior. A negative impact on self-esteem would be more risk-averse than others and would be ready to resort to any behavior to cover the situation. Consequently, the person may attempt to distort the input information in order to have an attainable budget. Belkaoui accordingly tested the hypothesis that individuals given negative feedback about their self-esteem would introduce more bias into estimates than individuals given positive or neutral feedback about their self-esteem.[86] One week after taking a self-esteem test, subjects were provided with false feedback (either positive or negative) and neutral feedback about heir self-esteem score. They were then asked to make two budgeting decisions, first one cost estimate and then one sales estimates for a fictional budgeting decision. The results showed that, in general, the individuals who were provided with information that temporarily caused them to lower their self-esteem were more apt to distort input information than those who ere made to raise their self-esteem. It was concluded that, whereas slack budgeting may be consistent with generally low self-esteem feedback, it is inconsistent with generally high or neutral self-esteem feedback.

Toward a Theoretical Framework for Budgeting

A theoretical framework aimed at structuring knowledge about biasing behavior was proposed by Kari Lukka.[87] It contains an explanatory model for budgetary biasing and a model for budgetary biasing at the organizational level.

The explanatory model of budgetary biasing at the individual level draws from the management accounting and organizational behavior literature and related behavioral research to suggest a set of intentions and determinants of budgetary biasing. Budgetary biasing is at the center of many interrelated and sometimes contradictory factors with the actor's intentions as the synthetic core of his or her behavior.

The model for budgetary biasing at organizational level shows that the "bias contained in the final budget is not the result of one actor's intentional behavior, but rather the result of the dialectics of the negotiations."[88] Whereas budgetary biases 1 and 2 are the original biases created in the budget by the controlling unit and the controlled unit, biases 3 and 4 are the final biases to end up in the budget after the budgetary negotiations, which are characterized by potential conflicts and power factors. The results of semistructured interviews at different levels of management of a large decentralized company verified the theoretical framework. The usefulness of this theoretical framework rests on further refinements and empirical testing.

Positive versus Negative Slack

Although the previous sections have focused on budgetary, or positive, slack, budgetary bias is, in fact, composed of both budgetary slack and an upward bias, or a negative slack. Whereas budgetary slack refers to bias in which the budget is designed intentionally so as to make it easier to achieve the forecast, upward bias refers to overstatement of expected performance in the budget. David T. Otley has described the difference as follows: "Managers are therefore likely to be conservative in making forecasts when future benefits are sought (positive slack) but optimistic when their need for obtaining current approval dominates (negative slack)."[89]

Evidence for negative slack was first provided by W.H. Read, who showed that managers distort information to prove to their superiors that all is well.[90] He cited several empirical studies of budgetary control that indicated that managers put a lot of effort and ingenuity into assuring that messages conveyed by budgetary information serve their own interests.[91] Following earlier research by Barefield, Otley argued that forecasts may be the mode, rather than the means, of people's intuitive probability distributions.[92] Given that the distribution of cost and revenue is negatively skewed, there will be a tendency for budget forecasts to become unintentionally biased in the form of negative slack. Data collected from two organizations verified the presence of negative slack.

Reducing Budgetary Slack: A Bonus-Based Technique

In general, firms use budgeting and bonus techniques to overcome slack budgeting. One such approach consists of paying higher rewards when budgets are set high and achieved and lower rewards when budgets are either set high but not met or set low and achieved. G.S. Mann presented a bonus system that gave incentives for managers to set budget estimates as close to achievable levels as possible.[100] The following two formulas were proposed:

> Formula 1 applies for bonus if actual performance is equal to or greater than budget.
>
> (multiplier no. 2 x budget goal) + [multiplier no.1 x (actual level achieved – budget goal)]

> Formula 2 applies for bonus if actual performance is less than budget.
>
> (multiplier no. 2 x budget goal) + [multiplier no.3 x (actual level achieved – budget goal)]

The three multipliers set by management served as factors in calculating different components of bonuses. They were defined as follows:

Multiplier no. 1 (which must be less than multiplier no. 2, and which in turn must be less than multiplier no.3) is used when actual performance is greater than budget. It provides a smaller bonus per unit for the part of actual performance that exceeds the budgeted amount...

Multiplier no. 2 is the rate per unit used to determine the basic bonus component. It is based on the budgeted level of activity which equals multiplier no. 2 times the budgeted level.

Multiplier no. 3 is the rate used to reduce the bonus when the chieved level is less than the budget (multiplier no. 3 times work of units by which actual performance fell short of budget).[94]

Exhibit 5.1 shows an illustration of the application of the method and the effect of variations in multipliers or bonuses. As the figure shows, the manager will be rewarded for accurate estimation of the level of rates. In addition, the multipliers can be set with greater flexibility for controlling the manager's estimates.

Exhibit 5.1

Reducing Slack through a Bonus System

(1)	(2)	(3)	(4) Bonus I	(5) Bonus II
Budget Sales	Actual Sales	State of Nature	Multiplier No. 1 = $.05 Multiplier No. 2 = $.10 Multiplier No. 3 = $.15	Multiplier No. 1 = $.01 Multiplier No. 2 = $.10 Multiplier No. 3 = $.30
200,000	180,000	Overestimation	$17,000	$14,000
200,000	200,000	Actual = Budget	20,000	20,000
200,000	220,000	Underestimation	21,000	22,000

CONCLUSION

Organizational slack and budgetary slack are two hypothetical constructs to explain organizational phenomena that are prevalent in all forms of organizations. Evidence linking both constructs to organizational, individual, and contextual factors is growing and in the future may contribute to an emerging theoretical framework for an understanding of slack. Further investigation into the potential determinants of organizational and budgetary slack remains to be done. This effort is an important one because the behavior of slack is highly relevant to the achievement of internal economic efficiency in organizations. Witness the following comment: "The effective organization has more rewards at its disposal, or more organizational slack to play with, and thus can allow all members to exercise more discretion, obtain more rewards, and feel that their influence is higher.[95]

NOTES

1. Richard M. Cyert and James G. March, eds., *A Behavioral Theory of the Firm* (Englewood Cliffs, NJ: Prentice-Hall, 1963).

2. Arie Y. Lewin and Carl Wolf, "The Theory of Organizational Slack: A Critical Review," *Proceedings: Twentieth International Meeting of TIMS* (1976), 648-54.

3. Harvey Leibenstein, "Allocative Efficiency vs. X-Efficiency," *American Economic Review* (June 1966), 392-415.

4. Harvey Leibenstein, "X-Efficiency; From Concept to Theory," *Challenge* (September-October 1979), 13-22.

5. Nandan Choudhury, "Incentives for the Divisional Manager," *Accounting and Business Research* (Winter 1985), 11-21.

6. S. Baiman, "Agency Research in Managerial Accounting: A Survey." *Journal of Accounting Literature* (Spring 1982), pp.154-213.

7. Packard, *The Pyramid Climber* (New York: McGraw-Hill, 1962); E.A. Butler, "Corporate Politics-Monster or Friend?" *Generation* 3 (1971), pp.54-58, 74; A.N. Schoomaker, *Executive Career Strategies* (New York: American Management Association, 1971).

8. J. Pfeffer, "Power and Resource Allocation in Organizations," in B.M. Shaw and G.R. Salancik (eds.), *New Directions in Organizational Behavior* (Chicago: St. Clair Press, 1977).

9. V.E. Schein, "Individual Power and Political Behaviors in Organizations: An Inadequately Explored Reality," *Academy of Management Review* (January 1977), pp.64-72.

10. B. Bowman and W. Malpive, “Goals and Bureaucratic Decision-Making: An Experiment,” *Human Relations* (June 1977), pp.417-429.

11. V.E. Schein, “Examining an Illusion: The Role of Deceptive Behaviors in Organizations,” *Human Relations* (October 1979), pp.288-289.

12. Ibid., p.290.

13. Cyert and March, A Behavioral Theory of the Firm.

14. Schein, “Examining an Illusion,” p.293.

15. Cyert and March, A Behavioral Theory of the Firm.

16. John Child, “Organizational Structure, Environment, and Performance: The Role of Strategic Choice,” *Sociology* 6, 1 (1972), pp.2-22.

17. M.D. Cohen, J.G. March, and J.P. Olsen, “A Garbage Can Model of Organizational Choice,” *Administrative Science Quarterly* 17, 1 (1972), pp.1-25.

18. J.G. March and J.P. Olsen, *Ambiguity and Choice* (Bergen: Universitetsforlagt, 1976).

19. D.E. Dimmick and V.V. Murray, “Correlates of Substantive Policy Decisions in Organizations: The Case of Human Resource Management.” *Academy of Management Journal* 21, 4 (1978), pp. 611-623.

20. R.J. Litschert and T.W. Bonham, “A Conceptual Model of Strategy Formation,” *Academy of Management Review* 3, 2 (1978), pp.211-219.

21. James G. March, interview by Stanford Business School Alumni Association, *Stanford GSB* 47, 3 (1978-1979), pp.16-19.

22. Cyert and March, A Behavioral Theory of the Firm.

23. Ibid., p.38.

24. Oliver E. Williamson, "A Model of Rational Managerial Behavior," in Cyert and March, *A Behavioral Theory of the Firm*; O.E. Williamson, *The Economics of Discretionary Behavior: Managerial Objectives in a Theory of the Firm* (Englewood Cliffs, NJ: Prentice-Hall, 1964).

25. J.Y. Kamin and J. Ronen, "The Smoothing of Income Numbers: Some Empirical Evidence on Systematic Differences among Management-Controlled and Owner-Controlled Firms," *Accounting, Organizations and Society* (October 1978), pp.141-157.

26. Ahmed Belkaoui and R.D. Picur, "The Smoothing of Income Numbers: Some Empirical Evidence on Systematic Differences between Core and Periphery Industrial Sector," *Journal of Business Finance and Accounting* (Winter 1984), pp. 527-545.

27. Lewin and Wolf, "The Theory of Organizational Slack," p.653.

28. L.J. Bourgeois, "On the Measurement of Organizational Slack," *Academy of Management Review* 6, 1 (1981), pp.29-39.

29. Ibid., p.31.

30. C.I. Barnard, *Functions of the Executive* (Cambridge, MA: Harvard University Press, 1938).

31. James G. March and H.A. Simon, *Organizations* (New York: John Wiley and Sons, 1958).

32. Cyert and March, *A Behavioral Theory of the Firm*, p.36.

33. L.R. Pondy, "Organizational Conflict: Concepts and Models," *Administrative Science Quarterly* 12, 2 (1967), pp.296-320.

34. J.D. Thompson, *Organizations in Action* (New York: McGraw-Hill, 1967).

35. Pondy, "Organizational Conflict."

36. Jay Galbraith, *Designing Complex Organizations* (Reading, MA: Addison-Wesley, 1973), p.15.

37. Bourgeois, "On the Measurement of Organizational Slack," p.34.

38. D.C. Hambrick and C.C. Snow, "A Contextual Model of Strategic Decision Making in Organizations," in R.L. Taylor, J.J. O'Connell, R.A. Zawaki, and D.D. Warrick (eds.), *Academy of Management Proceedings* (1977), pp. 109-112.

39. Cyert and March, A Behavioral Theory of the Firm.

40. March and Simon, *Organizations.*

41. H.A. Simon, *Administrative Behavior* (New York: Free Press, 1957).

42. Cyert and March, A Behavioral Theory of the Firm.

43. W.G. Astley, "Sources of Power in Organizational Life" (Ph.D. diss., University of Washington, 1978).

44. W.Richard Scott, *Organizations: Rational, Natural and Open Systems* (Englewood Cliffs, NJ: Prentice-Hall, 1981), p.216.

45. Ibid.

46. Ibid.

47. Bourgeois, "On the Measurement of Organizational Slack," p.38.

48. Martin M. Rosner, "Economic Determinant of Organizational Innovation," *Administrative Science Quarterly* 12 (1968), pp.614-625.

49. Arie Y. Lewin and Carl Wolf, "Organizational Slack: A Test of the General Theory," *Journal of Management Studies* (forthcoming).

50. L.J. Bourgeois and Jitendra V. Singh, "Organizational Slack and Political Behavior within Top Management Teams," Working paper, Graduate School of Business, Stanford University, 1983.

51. Teresa K. Lant, "Modeling Organizational Slack: An Empirical Investigation," Stanford University Research Paper no.856, July 1986.

52. Ibid., p.14.

53. Michael Schiff and Arie Y. Lewin, "The Impact of People on Budget," *Accounting Review* (April 1970), pp.259-268.

54. Michael Schiff and Arie Y. Lewin, "Where Traditional Budgeting Fails," *Financial Executive* (May 1968), pp.51-62.

55. A.E. Lowe and R.W. Shaw. "An Analysis of Managerial Biasing Evidence from a Company's Budgeting Process," *Journal of Management Studies* (October 1968), pp.304-315.

56. M. Dalton, *Men Who Manage* (New York: John Wiley and Sons, 1961), pp.36-38.

57. Shillinglaw, "Divisional Performance Review: An Extension of Budgetary Control," in C.P. Bonini, R.K. Jaedicke, and H.M. Wagner (eds.), *Management Controls: New Directors in Basic Research* (New York: McGraw-Hill, 1964), pp.149-163.

58. C. Argyris, *The Impact of Budgets on People* (New York: Controllership Foundation, 1952), p.25.

59. E.H. Caplan, *Management Accounting and Behavioral Sciences* (Reading, MA: Addison-Wesley, 1971).

60. Argyris, The Impact of Budgets on People.

61. Schiff and Lewin, "Where Traditional Budgeting Fails," pp.51-62.

62. Mohamed Onsi, "Factor Analysis of Behavioral Variables Affecting Budgetary Slack," *Accounting Review* (July 1973), pp.535-548.

63. Ibid., p.536.

64. Ibid., p.539.

65. Ibid., p.546.

66. Cortlandt Cammann, "Effects of the Use of Control Systems," *Accounting Organizations and Society* (January 1976), pp.301-313.

67. Kenneth A. Merchant, "Budgeting and the Propensity to Create Budgetary Slack," *Accounting, Organizations and Society* (May 1985), pp.201-210.

68. Alan S. Dunk, "The Effect of Budget Emphasis and Information Asymmetry on the Relation between Budgetary Participation and Slack," *The Accounting Review* (April 1993), pp.400-410.

69. Ibid., p.400.

70. Ibid., pp.408-409.

71. Richard M. Cyert, J.G. March, and W.H. Starbuck, "Two Experiments on Bias and Conflict in Organizational Estimation," *Management Science* (April 1961), pp.254-264.

72. Lowe and Shaw, "An Analysis of Managerial Biasing."

73. Delton, Men Who Manage.

74. R.M. Barefield, "A Model of Forecast Biasing Behavior," *Accounting Review* (July 1970), pp.490-501.

75. J.S. Demski and G.A. Feltham, "Economic Incentives in Budgetary Control Systems," *Accounting Review* (April 1978), pp.336-359.

76. Y. Ijiri, J. Kinard, and F. Purney, "An Integrated Evaluation System for Budget Forecasting and Operating Performance with a Classified Budgeting Bibliography," *Journal of Accounting Research* (Spring 1968), pp.1-28; M. Loeb and W. Magat, "Soviet Success Indicators and the Evaluation of Divisional Performance," *Journal of Accounting Research* (Spring 1978), pp.103=121; P. Jennergren, "On the Design of Incentives in Business Firms — A Survey of Some Research," *Management Science* (February 1980), pp.180-201; M. Weitzman, "The New Soviet Incentive Model," *Bell Journal of Economics* (Spring 1976), pp.251-257.

77. Mark S. Young, "Participative Budgeting: The Effects of Risk Aversion and Asymmetric Information on Budgetary Slack," *Journal of Accounting Research* (Autumn 1985), pp.829-842.

78. Ibid., pp.831-832.

79. C. Chow, J. Cooper, and W. Waller, "Participative Budgeting: Effects of a Truth-Inducing Pay Scheme and Information Asymmetry on Slack and Performance," Working paper, University of Arizona, Tucson, 1986.

80. William S. Waller, “Slack in Participative Budgeting: The Joint Effect of a Truth-Inducing Pay Scheme and Risk Preferences,” *Accounting, Organizations and Society* (December 1987), pp.87-98.

81. Ibid., p.88.

82. J. Berg, L. Daley, J. Dickhaut, and J. O’Brien, “Controlling Preferences for Lotteries on Units of Experimental Exchange,” *Quarterly Journal of Economics* (May 1986), pp.281-306.

83. D.C. Kim, “Risk Preferences in Participative Budgeting,” *The Accounting Review* (April 1992), pp.303-318.

84. Ibid., p.304.

85. E. Aronson and D.R. Mettee, “Dishonest Behavior as a Function of Differential Levels of Induced Self-Esteem,” *Journal of Personality and Social Psychology* (January 1968), pp.121-127.

86. Ahmed Belkaoui, “Slack Budgeting, Information Distortion and Self-Esteem,” *Contemporary Accounting Research* (Fall 1985), pp.111-123.

87. Kari Lukka, “Budgetary Biasing in Organizations: Theoretical Framework and Empirical Evidence,” *Accounting, Organizations and Society* (February 1988), pp.281-301.

88. Ibid., p.292.

89. David T. Otley, “The Accuracy of Budgetray Estimates: Some Statistical Evidence,” *Journal of Business Finance and Accounting* (Fall 1985), p.416.

90. W.H. Read, “Upward Communication in Industrial Hierarchies,” *Human Relations* (1962), pp.3-16.

91. G.H. Hofstede, *The Game of Budget Control* (London: Tavistock, 1968); A.G. Hopwood, "An empirical Study of the Role of Accounting Data in Performance Evaluation," *Journal of Accounting Research* (Supplement, 1972), pp.156-182; D.T. Otley, "Budget Use and Managerial Performance," *Journal of Accounting Research* (Spring 1978), pp.122-149.

92. R.M. Barefield, "Comments on a Measure of Forecasting Performance," *Journal of Accounting Research* (Autumn 1969), pp.324-327; Otley, "The Accuracy of Budgetary Estimates."

93. G.S. Mann, "Reducing Budget Slack," *Journal of Accountancy* (August 1988), pp.18-122.

94. Ibid., p.119.

95. Charles Perrow, *Complex Organizations: A Critical Essay* (Glenview, IL: Scott, Foreman, and Company, 1972), p.140.

SELECTED BIBLIOGRAPHY

Antle, R., and G. Eppen. "Capital Rationing and Organizational Slack in Capital Budgeting." *Management Science* (February 1985), pp.163-174.

Argyris, C. *The Impact of Budgets on People.* New York: Controllership Foundation, 1952.

Aronson, E., and D.R. Mettee. "Dishonest Behavior as a Function of Differential Levels of Induced Self-Esteem." *Journal of Personality and Social Psychology* (January 1968), pp.121-127.

Astley, W.G. "Sources of Power in Organizational Life." Ph.D.diss., University of Washington, 1978.

Barefield, R.M. "A Model of Forecast Biasing Behavior." *Accounting Review* (July 1970), pp.490-501.

Barnard, C.I. *Functions of the Excutive.* Cambridge, MA: Harvard University Press, 1937.

Bernea, A., J. Ronen, and S. Sadan. "Classifactory Smoothing of Income with Extraordinary Items." *Accounting Review* (January 1976), pp.110-122.

Belkaoui, A. Conceptual Foundations of Management Accounting. Reading, MA: Addison-Wesley, 1980.

———. Cost Accounting: A Multidimensional Emphasis. Hinsdale, IL: Dryden Press, 1983.

———. "The Relationships between Self-Disclosure Style and Attitudes to Responsibility Accounting." *Accounting, Organizations and Society* (December 1981), pp.281-289.

———. "Slack Budgeting, Information Distortion and Self-Esteem." *Contemporary Accounting Research* (Fall 1985), pp.111-123.

Belkaoui, A., and R.D. Picur. "The Smoothing of Income Numbers: Some Empirical Evidence of Systematic Differences between Core and Periphery Industrial Sectors." *Journal of Business Finance and Accounting* (Winter 1984), pp.527-545.

Bonin, J.P. "On the Decision of Managerial Incentive Structures in a Decentralized Planning Environment." *American Economic Review* (September 1976): 682-87.

Bonin, J.P., and A. Marcus. "Information, Motivation, and Control in Decentralized Planning: The Case of Discretionary Managerial Behavior." *Journal of Comparative Economics* (September 1979): 235-53.

Bourgeois, L.J. "On the Measurement of Organizational Slack." *Academy of Management Review* 6, no. 1 (1981), pp.29-39.

Bourgeois, L.J. and W.G. Astley, "A Strategic Model of Organizational Conduct and Performance." *International Studies of Management and Organization* 9, 3 (1979), pp.40-66.

Bourgeois, L.J., and J.V. Singh. "Organizational Slack and Political Behavior within Top Management Teams." Working paper, Graduate School of Business, Stanford University, 1983.

Brownell, P. "Participation in the Budgeting Process — When It Works and When It Doesn't." *Journal of Accounting Literature* (Spring 1982), pp.124-153.

Caplan, E.H. *Management Accounting and Behavioral Sciences.* Reading, MA: Addison-Wesley, 1971.

Carter, E. "The Behavioral Theory of the Firm and Top-Level Corporate Decisions." *Administrative Science Quarterly* 16, 4 (1971), pp.413-428.

Child, J. "Organizational Structure, Environment, and Performance: The Role of Strategic Choice." *Sociology* 6, 1 (1972), pp.2-22.

Chow, C., J. Cooper, and W. Waller. "Participative Budgeting: Effects of a Truth-Inducing Pay Scheme and Information Asymmetry on Slack and Performance." Working paper. University of Arizona, Tucson, 1986.

Chow, D. "The Effects of Job Standard Tightness and Compensation Scheme on Performance: An Exploration of Linkages." *Accounting Review* (October 1983), pp.667-685.

Christensen, J. "The Determination of Performance Standards and Participation." *Journal of Accounting Research* (Autumn 1982), pp.589-603.

Cohen, M.D., J.G. March, and J.P. Olsen, "A Garbage Can Model of Organizational Choice." *Administrative Science Quarterly* 17, 1 (1972), pp.1-25.

Collins, F. "Managerial Accounting Systems and Organizational Control: A Role Perspective." *Accounting, Organizations and Society* (May 1982), pp.107-122.

Conn, D. "A Comparison of Alternative Incentive Structures for Centrally Planned Economic Systems." *Journal of Comparative Economics* (September 1979), pp.261-278.

Cyert, Richard M., ed. *A Behavioral Theory of the Firm.* Englewood Cliffs, NJ: Prentice-Hall, 1963.

Cyert, Richard M., and J.G. March. "Organizational Factors in the Theory of Oligopoly." *Quarterly Journal of Economics* (April 1956), pp.44-66.

Cyert, R.M., J.G. March, and W.H. Starbuck. "Two Experiments on Bias and Conflict in Organizational Estimation." *Management Science* (April 1961), pp.254-264.

Dalton, M. *Men Who Manage.* New York: John Wiley and Sons, 1961.

Demski, J.S., and G.A. Feltham. "Economic Incentives in Budgetary Control Systems." *Accounting Review* (April 1978), pp.336-359.

Dimmick, D.E., and V.V. Murray. "Correlates of Substantive Policy Decisions in Organizations: The Case of Human Resource Management." *Academy of Management Journal* 21, no. 4 (1978): 611-23.

Dunk, A.S. "The Effect of Budget Emphasis and Information Asymmetry on the Relation between Budgetary Participation and Slack." *The Accounting Review* (April 1993), pp.400-410.

Fitts, W.F. Manual for the Tennessee Self-Concept Scale. Nashville, TN: Counselor Recording and Tests, 1965.

———. Interpersonal Competence: The Wheel Model. Nashville, TN: Counselor Recording and Tests, 1970.

———. The Self-Concept and Behavior: Overview and Supplement. Nashville, TN: Counselor Recording and Tests, 1972.

———. The Self-Concept and Performance. Nashville, TN: Counselor Recording and Tests, 1972.

———. The Self-Concept and Psychopathology. Nashville, TN: Counselor Recording and Tests, 1972.

Fitts, W.F., J.L. Adams, G. Radford, W.C. Richard, B.K. Thomas, M.M. Thomas, and W. Thompson. The Self-Concept and Self-Actualization. Nashville, TN: Counselor Recording and Tests, 1971.

Fitts, W.F., and W.T. Hammer. The Self-Concept and Delinquency. Nashville, TN: Counselor Recording and Tests, 1969.

Galbraith, Jay. *Designing Complex Organizations.* Reading, MA: Addison-Wesley, 1973.

Gonik, J. "Tie Salesmen's Bonuses to Their Forecasts." *Harvard Business Review* (May-June 1978), pp.116-123.

Gordon, M.J., B.N.Horwitz, and P.T. Myers. "Accounting Measurements and Normal Growth of the Firm." In *Research in Accounting Measurement,* ed. R.K. Jaedicke, Y. Ijiri, and O. Nieslen. Sarasota, FL: American Accounting Association, 1966.

Hambrick, D.C., and C.C. Snow. "A Contextual Model of Strategic Decision Making in Organizations." In *Academy of Management Proceedings,* ed. R.L. Taylor, J. J. O'Connell, R. A. Zawacki, and D.D. Warrick (1977): 109-12.

Hershey, J., H. Kunreuther, and P. Shoemaker. "Bias in Assessment Procedures for Utility Functions." *Management Science* (August 1982): 936-54.

Hopwood, A.G. "An Empirical Study of the Role of Accounting Data in Performance Evaluation." *Journal of Accounting Research* (Supplement, 1972), pp.156-182.

Irjiri, Y., J. Kinard, and F. Putney. "An Integrated Evaluation System for Budget Forecasting and Operating Performance with a Classified Budgeting Bibliography." *Journal of Accounting Research* (Spring 1968), pp.1-28.

Itami, H. "Evaluation Measures and Goal Congruence under Uncertainty." *Journal o f Accounting Research* (Spring 1975), pp.163-180.

Jennergren, p. "On the Design of Incentives in Business Firms – A Survey of Some Research." *Management Science* (February 1980), pp.180-201.

Kamin, J.Y., and J. Ronen. "The Smoothing of Income Numbers: Some Empirical Evidence on Systematic Differences among Management-Controlled and Owner-Controlled Firms." *Accounting, Organizations and Society* (October 1978): 141-57.

Kerr, S., and W. Slocum Jr. "Controlling the Performances of People in Organizations." In W. Starbuck and P. Nystrom (eds.), *Handbook of Organizational Design,* Vol. 2. New York: Oxford University Press, 1981, pp. 116-134.

Kim, D.C. "Risk Preferences in Participative Budgeting." *The Accounting Review* (April 1992), pp.303-319.

Lecky, P. *Self-Consistency.* New York: Island Press, 1945.

Leibenstein, H. "Allocative Efficiency vs. X-Efficiency." *American Economic Review* (June 1996), pp.392-415.

———. "X-Efficiency: From Concept to Theory." *Challenge* (September-October 1979), pp.13-22.

Levinthal, D., and J.G. March. "A Model of Adaptive Organizational Search." *Journal of Economic Behavior and Organization* (May 1981), pp.307-333.

Lewin, Arie Y. "Organizational Slack: A Test of the General Theory." *Journal of Management Studies* (forthcoming).

Lewin, Arie Y., and Carl Wolf. "The Theory of Organizational Slack: A Critical Review." *Proceedings: Twentieth International Meeting of TIMS* (1976), pp.648-654.

Litschert, R.J., and T.W. Bonham. "A Conceptual Model of Strategy Formation." *Academy of Management Review* 3, 2 (1978), pp.211-219.

Locke, E., and D. Schweiger. "Participation in Decision Making: One More Look." In B. Staw (ed.), *Research in Organizational Behavior.* Greenwich, CT: JAI Press, 1979, pp.265-339.

Loeb, M., and W. Magat. "Soviet Success Indicators and the Evaluation of Divisional Performance." *Journal of Accounting Research* (Spring 1978), pp.103-121.

Lowe, A.E., and R.W. Shaw. "An Analysis of Managerial Biasing: Evidence from a Company's Budgeting Process." *Journal of Management Studies* (October 1968), pp.304-315.

March, James G. "Decisions in Organizations and Theories of Choice." In *Perspectives on Organizational Design and Behavior,* ed. Andrew H. Van de Ven and William F. Joyce. New York: Wiley, 1981, 215-35.

———. "Interview by Stanford Business School Alumni Association," *Stanford CSB* 47, no. 3 (1978-1979): 16-19.

March, James G., and H.A. Simon. *Organizations.* New York: John Wiley and Sons, 1958.

Merchant, Kenneth A. "The Design of the Corporate Budgeting System: Influences on Managerial Behavior and Performance." *The Accounting Review* (October 1981): 813-29.

Mezias, Stephen J. "Some Analytics of Organizational Slack." Working paper, Graduate School of Business, Stanford University, November 1985.

Miller, J., and J.Thompson. "Effort, Uncertainty, and the New Soviet Incentive System." *Southern Economic Journal* (October 1978), pp.432-446.

Mitroff, I.I., and J.R. Emshoff. "On Strategic Assumption-Making: A Dialectical Approach to Policy and Planning." *Academy of Management Review* 4, 1 (1979), pp.1-12.

Moch, M.K., and L.R. Pondy. "The Structure of Chaos: Organized Anarchy as a Response to Ambiguity." *Administrative Science Quarterly* 22, 2 (1977), pp.351-362.

Onsi, Mohamed. "Factor Analysis of Behavioral Variables Affecting Budgetary Slack." *The Accounting Review* (July 1973), pp.535-548.

Parker, L.D. "Goal Congruence: A Misguided Accounting Concept." *Abacus* (June 1976), pp.3-13.

Pondy, L.R. "Organizational Conflict: Concepts and Models." *Administrative Science Quarterly* 12, no. 2 (1967): 296-320.

Radnor, R. "A Behavioral Model of Cost Reduction." *Bell Journal of Economics* (Fall 1975): 196-215.

Rogers, C.R. *Client Centered Therapy.* Boston: Houghton Miffin, 1951.

Rosner, Martin M. “Economic Determinant of Organizational Innovation.” *Administrative Science Quarterly* 12 (1968): 614-25.

Schein, V.E. “Examining an Illusion: The Role of Deceptive Behaviors in Organizations.” *Human Relations* (October 1979), pp.287-295.

Schiff, M. “Accounting Tactics and the Theory of the Firm.” *Journal of Accounting Research* (Spring 1966), pp.62-67.

Schiff, Michael, and Arie Y. Levin. *Behavioral Aspects of Accounting.* Englewood Cliffs, NJ: Prentice-Hall, 1974.

——. “The Impact of People on Budgets.” *Accounting Review* (April 1970), pp.259-268.

——. “Where Traditional Budgeting Fails.” *Financial Executive* (May 1968), pp.51-62.

Simon, H.A. *Administrative Behavior.* New York: Free Press, 1957.

Singh, Jitendra V. “Performance, Slack and Risk Taking in Organizational Decision Making.” *Academy of Management Journal* (September 1986): 562-85.

——. “Performance, Slack, and Risk Taking in Strategic Decisions: Test of a Structural Equation Model.” Ph.D. diss., Stanford Graduate School of Business, 1983.

Snygg, D., and A.W. Combs. *Individual Behavior.* New York: Harper and Row, 1949.

Staw, B.M. “Rationality and Justification in Organizational Life.” In *Research in Organizational Behavior,* vol. 2, ed. B.M. Staw and L.L. Cummings. Greenwich, CT: JAI Press, 1980, 154-82.

Swieringa, R.J., and R.H. Moncur. "The Relationship between Managers' Budget Oriented Behavior and Selected Attitudes, Position, Size and Performance Measures." *Journal of Accounting Research* (Supplement, 1972), p.19.

Thompson, J.D. *Organizations in Action.* New York: McGraw-Hill, 1967.

Thompson, W. *Correlates of the Self-Concept.* Nashville, TN: Counselor Recording and Tests, 1972.

Waller, Williams S., and C. Chow. "The Self-Selection and Effort of Standard-Based Employment Contracts: A Framework and Some Empirical Evidence." *Accounting Review* (July 1985), pp.458-476.

Weitzman, M. "The New Soviet Incentive Model." *Bell Journal of Economics* (Spring 1976), pp.251-257.

Williamson, Oliver E. *The Economics of Discretionary Behavior: Managerial Objectives in a Theory of the Firm.* Englewood Cliffs, NJ: Prentice-Hall, 1964.

———. "A Model of Rational Managerial Behavior." In Richard M. Cyert and James G. March (eds.), *A Behavioral Theory of the Firm.* Englewood Cliffs, NJ: Prentice-Hall, 1963, pp.113-128.

Winter, Sidney G. "Satisficing, Selection, and the Innovating Remnant." *Quarterly Journal of Economics* 85 (1971), pp.237-257.

Woot, P.D., H. Heyvaert, and F. Martou. "Strategic Management: An Empirical Study of 168 Belgian Firms." *International Studies of Management and Organization* 7 (1977): 60-73.

Wylie, R.C. *The Self-Concept: A Critical Survey of Pertinent Research Literature*. Lincoln: University of Nebraska Press, 1961.

Young, Mark S. "Participative Budgeting: The Effects of Risk Aversion and Asymmetric Information on Budgetary Slack." *Journal of Accounting Research* (Autumn 1985), pp.829-842.

ABOUT THE AUTHOR

Ahmed Riahi-Belkaoui is an Emeritus Professor at the University of Illinois at Chicago. Previously, he was named University Scholar at UIC (2000-2003), CBA Distinguished professor (1996-2001), 2000 AAA outstanding International Educator, and founding editor of the Review of Accounting and Finance (2001-2007). His research interests embrace socio-economic accounting, behavioral accounting, and social and political issues. He has published over 78 books, including Social Status Matters, and Qaddafi: The man and His Policies, and more than one hundred eighty articles and reviews in major journals.

PUBLICATIONS

Books by Professor Ahmed Riahi-Belkaoui

1. FINANCIAL ACCOUNTING: THEORY AND ANALYSIS:

1. Elements de Theorie Comptable (Universite d'Ottawa, Departement de Commerce, 1974), pp.168

2. **Corporate Financial Disclosure in Canada**, Canadian Certified General Accountants Association, Monograph #1 (Vancouver, British Columbia, 1978), pp.63. (Co-author: Alfred Kahl).
3. **Theorie Comptable**, (Presses de L' Universite du Quebec, Quebec, 1984). 2nd Edition, pp. 416.
4. **Accounting Theory**, (International Thomson Publishing, 2004) 5th Edition.(Translated in Chinese, Habasa Indonesian, and Korean) pp.598
5. **Industrial Bond Ratings and the Rating Process** (Greenwood Publishing Group, 1983): 198.
6. **Inquiry and Accounting: Alternative Methods and Research Perspectives** (Greenwood Publishing Group, 1987): 355.
7. **Determinants of Executive Compensation: Ownership, Performance, Firm Size and Corporate Diversification** (Greenwood Publishing Group, 1991): 163. Co-author: Ellen Pavlik.
8. **Accounting in the Dual Economy** (Greenwood Publishing Group, 1991): 159.
9. **Accounting: A Multiple Paradigm Science** (Greenwood Publishing Group, 1996)
10. **Accounting Theory: The Australian** Edition (Harcourt, 3rd Edition, 2005)
11. **Critical Financial Accounting Problems: Issues and Solutions** (Greenwood Publishing Group, 1998)

12. **Research Perspectives in Accounting** (Greenwood Publishing Group, 1997)

13. **Financial Analysis and the Predictability of Important Economic Events** (Greenwood Publishing Group, 1998)

14. **Capital Structure: Determination, Evaluation and Accounting** (Greenwood Publishing Group, 1999)

15. **Earnings Measurement, Determination, Management and Usefulness** (Greenwood Publishing, 1999)

16. **Accounting and the Investment Opportunity Set** (Greenwood Publishing Group, 2000).

17. **Financial Statements: Present and Future Scope** (Greenwood Publishing Group, 2001).

18. **Accounting: Principled or Designed** (Greenwood Publishing, 2003)

19. **Earnings Interrupted** (Create Space, 2011)

20. **Finding Value** (Create Space 2010)

2. PUBLIC POLICY AND PUBLIC INTEREST ACCOUNTING.

1. **Socio-Economic Accounting** (Greenwood Publishing Group, 1984).

2. **Public Policy and the Problems and Practices of Accounting** (Greenwood Publishing, 1985): 204.

3. **The Coming Crisis in Accounting** (Greenwood Publishing Group, 1989).

4. **Accounting for Corporate Reputation** (Greenwood Publishing Group, 1992). Co-author: Ellen Pavlik.

5. **Morality in Accounting** (Greenwood Publishing Group, 1992).

6. **Human Resource Valuation** (Greenwood Publishing Group, 1995). Co-author: Janice Monti-Belkaoui.

7. **Fairness in Accounting** (Greenwood Publishing Group, 1996) Co-author: Janice Monti-Belkaoui.

8. **Corporate Social Awareness and Financial Outcomes** (Greenwood Publishing Group, 1999).

9. **Wealth and Value Added: Reporting, Analysis and Taxation** (Book surge, 2010)

3. MANAGEMENT ACCOUNTING.

1. **The Conceptual Foundations of Management Accounting** (Addison Wesley, 1980).

2. **Cost Accounting : A Multidimensional Emphasis** (Dryden Press, 1983): 636.

3. **The Learning Curve: A Management Accounting Tool** (Greenwood Publishing Group, 1986): 245.

4. **Handbook of Management Control Systems** (Greenwood Publishing Group, 1986): 355.

5. **Quantitative Models in Accounting: A Guide to Practitioners** (Greenwood Publishing, 1987): 355.

6. **Handbook of Cost Accounting: Theory and Techniques** (Greenwood Publishing Group, 1991): 381.

7. **The New Foundations of Management Accounting** (Greenwood Publishing Group, 1992).

8. **Quality and Control: An Accounting Perspective** (Greenwood Publishing Group, 1992).

9. **Organizational and Budgetary Slack** (Greenwood Publishing Group, 1994)

10. **The Nature and Consequences of the Multidivisional Structure** (Greenwood Publishing, 1995)

11. **Long term Leasing: Accounting, Evaluation and Consequences** (Greenwood Publishing, 1998)

12. **Advanced Management Accounting** (Greenwood Publishing, 2001)

13. **Evaluating Capital Projects** (Greenwood Publishing 2001)

4. INTERNATIONAL ACCOUNTING

1. **International Accounting** (Greenwood Publishing Group, 1985).

2. **The New Environment in International Accounting: Issues and Practices** (Greenwood Publishing Group, 1987): 220.

3. **Judgement in International Accounting** (Greenwood Publishing Group, 1990).

4. **Multinational Management Accounting** (Greenwood Publishing Group, 1991).

5. **Multinational Financial Accounting** (Greenwood Publishing Group, 1991).

6. **Value Added Reporting: The Lessons for the U.S**. (Greenwood Publishing Group, 1992): 165.

7. **Accounting for the Developing Countries** (Greenwood Publishing Group, 1994)

8. **International and Multinational Accounting** (Dryden Press, 1994).

9. **The Cultural Shaping of Accounting** (Greenwood Press, 1995).

10. **The Linguistic Shaping of Accounting** (Greenwood Press, 1995).

11. **Performance Results in Value Added Reporting** (Greenwood Publishing Group, 1996).

12. **Multinationality and Financial Performance** (Greenwood Publishing Group, 1996).

13. **Disclosure Adequacy: Nature and Determinants** (Greenwood Publishing Group, 1997).

14. **Significant Current Issues in International Taxation** (Greenwood Publishing Group, 1998).

15. **The Nature, Estimation and Management of Political Risk** (Greenwood Publishing Group, 1998).

16. **Performance Results of Multinationality** (Greenwood Publishing Group, 1999).

17. **Value Added Reporting and Research** (Greenwood Publishing Group, 1999).

18. **The Role of Corporate Reputation for Multinational Firms: Accounting, Organizational and Market Considerations** (Greenwood Publishing Group, 2001)

19. **International Financial and Managerial Accounting** (Greenwood Publishing Group, 2002)

20. **Multinationality: Earnings, Efficiency and Market Considerations** (Greenwood Publishing Group, 2002).

21. **International Accounting and Economic Development: The Interactions of Economic and Social Indicators** (Greenwood Publishing, 2002)

5. BEHAVIORAL ACCOUNTING

1. **Behavioral Accounting** (Greenwood Publishing Group, 1989).

2. **Human Information Processing** (Greenwood Publishing Group, 1989).

3. **Behavioral Management Accounting** (Greenwood Publishing Group, 2002).

6. SOCIOLOGY

1. **Social Status Matters** (Booksurge, 2009).

7. FICTION, NONFICTION AND OTHER BOOKS

1. **Sherazade and Her Two Lovers** (Catskill, NY: Press-Tige Publishing Inc 1996)
2. **Like a Firm Knot in a Rope** (Chicago; A.D. Press, 2001) also published as .The Baraka (Catskill, NY: Press-Tige Publishing Inc 1997)
3. **Qaddafi: The Man and His Policies** (Gower House, Ashgate Publishing, Avebury, 1996)
4. **So You Want to Be Sophisticated** (Catskill, NY: Press-Tige Publishing Inc 1997)
5. **Conjugal Blues** .(Catskill, NY; Press-Tige Press, 1999)
6. **Shame** (Huntington, WV: Aegina Press, 1998)
7. **Written (Mektoub)** (Thomaston, ME: Century Press, 2000).
8. **Putting on the Dog: Guide to American Sophistication** (American Literary Press, 2004)
9. **Love and Obsession in Chicago** (Booksurge. 2009)
10. **On The Wrong Side of Chicago Beds: A Tale of Lust, Art and Politics** (Booksurge. 2009)
11. **How to Become Sophisticated** (Booksurge. 2009)